...tablished
...el brands,
... in travel.

...years our
guidebooks have unlocked the secrets
of destinations around the world,
sharing with travellers a wealth of
experience and a passion for travel.

**Rely on Thomas Cook as your
travelling companion on your next trip
and benefit from our unique heritage.**

Thomas Cook **pocket** guides

BELGRADE
Debbie Stowe

Thomas
Cook

Written and updated by Debbie Stowe
Original photography by Vasile Szakacs

Published by Thomas Cook Publishing
A division of Thomas Cook Tour Operations Limited
Company registration no. 3772199 England
The Thomas Cook Business Park, Unit 9, Coningsby Road,
Peterborough PE3 8SB, United Kingdom
Email: books@thomascook.com, Tel: +44 (0) 1733 416477
www.thomascookpublishing.com

Produced by Cambridge Publishing Management Limited
Burr Elm Court, Main Street, Caldecote CB23 7NU
www.cambridgepm.co.uk

ISBN: 978-1-84848-550-1

© 2007, 2009 Thomas Cook Publishing
This third edition © 2012
Text © Thomas Cook Publishing
Maps © Thomas Cook Publishing/PCGraphics (UK) Limited
Transport map © Communicarta Limited

Series Editor: Karen Beaulah
Production/DTP: Steven Collins

Printed and bound in Spain by GraphyCems

Cover photography © yui/Shutterstock

CONTENTS

INTRODUCING BELGRADE

Introduction 6
When to go 8
Belgrade Summer Festival........12
History...14
Lifestyle..16
Culture 18

MAKING THE MOST OF BELGRADE

Shopping..22
Eating & drinking.......................25
Entertainment & nightlife......29
Sport & relaxation 32
Accommodation...........................34
The best of Belgrade 40
Suggested itineraries 42
Something for nothing 44
When it rains................................46
On arrival..48

THE CITY OF BELGRADE

Kalemegdan Fortress
  & around 58
Trg Republike &
  city centre 76
South Belgrade 88

OUT OF TOWN TRIPS

Novi Beograd & Zemun..........102
Belgrade to Novi Sad 114

PRACTICAL INFORMATION

Directory 126
Emergencies...................................136

INDEX 138

MAPS

Belgrade..50
Belgrade transport map...........54
Kalemegdan Fortress
  & around 60
Trg Republike &
  city centre 78
South Belgrade............................90
Belgrade region 104

SYMBOLS KEY

The following symbols are used throughout this book:

ⓐ address ☎ telephone ⓦ website address ⓔ email
🕓 opening times Ⓝ public transport connections ❶ important

The following symbols are used on the maps:

𝒊	information office	▦	point of interest
✈	airport	◯	city
✚	hospital	○	large town
🛡	police station	○	small town
🚌	bus station	=	motorway
🚆	railway station	—	main road
Ⓜ	metro	—	minor road
✝	cathedral	—	railway
❶	numbers denote featured cafés & restaurants		

Hotels and restaurants are graded by approximate price as follows:
£ budget price **££** mid-range price **£££** expensive

▶ *A symbol of Serbia's struggles: the Parliament building*

INTRODUCING
Belgrade

Introduction

Wandering around Belgrade's relaxed Old Town, with its chic restaurants, galleries and boutiques, it's almost impossible to imagine that just under 15 years ago the city was suffering a NATO bombardment. Today the Serbian capital is generally a serene metropolis, particularly as two of its main districts are pedestrianised – the Roman-era streets around Knez Mihailova, home to many of the city's best shops, eateries and museums, and the bohemian restaurant district Skadarlija. Despite – or perhaps because of – what they have endured over the years, Belgrade's citizens now seem focused on life's simple pleasures, socialising at the many tiny bars and clubs dotted around, shopping or just sitting and watching the world go by in a café or in Trg Republike.

Small and easy to get around, and not too touristy, Belgrade strikes a balance that is ideal for the traveller who is adventurous enough to want to go somewhere new, but doesn't want to give up decent restaurants and other comforts. Visit this city and you'll be seeing it on the cusp of its transformation into a bustling centre of tourism and commerce. As a holiday destination, Belgrade ticks all the boxes. It's positively brimming with culture – not only is the city a living historical site in itself, but it boasts museums on everything from African art and the football club Red Star Belgrade to the weird and wonderful gifts given to President Tito during his decades in power. There are plenty of pleasant outside spaces for strollers to enjoy, from the car-free centre to various city parks and gardens, topped off by the showpiece Kalemegdan Fortress and its park, a large green area popular with families, couples and walkers. And, after the sightseeing, there's a wealth of cafés, restaurants and bars in which to unwind or party until sunrise.

⬤ *Kalemegdan Fortress stands guard over Belgrade*

When to go

SEASONS & CLIMATE

Belgrade has a continental climate, and in summer and winter
the weather can be more extreme than in the UK. The hottest
months are July and August, when average temperatures reach
22°C (72°F). On around 30 days per year the mercury can creep
up to the 39°C (102°F) mark. Summer is followed by a long,
warm autumn lasting well into early November, making this
a good time to visit. Winters can be chilly, with temperatures
dipping into the low minus numbers: January is the coldest
month, with average temperatures just over 0°C (32°F). Autumn
and winter also see the arrival of the *kosava*, a southeasterly
wind that gives the city a good clean. Spring is shorter than
autumn, and sees the wettest weather, particularly in May and
June. Summer comes around suddenly.

Belgrade is a city made for walking and many of its attractions
are in the open air, so it's probably wise to avoid the harshest
winter months. Nevertheless, it's a beautiful place in the snow,
and a winter visit has its own incentives, such as the Christmas
and New Year festivities and fun activities such as ice-skating
in Trg Nikole Pasika.

ANNUAL EVENTS
January
Open Heart Street Streets are closed off for Belgrade's colourful
New Year carnival on 1 January, which features shows by local
actors. ⓐ Svetogorska and Makedonska ⓣ 011 306 1400
ⓦ www.tob.co.rs

February–April

International Film Festival (FEST) Belgrade goes movie mad in spring with this festival, which often features the big Oscar contenders, starting at the end of February. ☎ 011 334 6946 ⓦ www.fest.rs

Documentary and Short Film Festival Coming a month after FEST, its main competition is supplemented by retrospectives,

⬤ *Party nights: the Belgrade Beer Fest*

exhibitions, seminars and workshops. ❶ 011 334 6946
Ⓦ www.kratkimetar.rs

Days of Belgrade Both celebrating the city and reflecting on its chequered history, the festivities include parades, theatre, a museum night, an ancient crafts fair plus concerts, sporting events and exhibitions. ❶ 011 715 7453 Ⓦ www.beograd.rs

Belgrade Marathon The largest sporting event in Serbia is based on a race from Obrenovac to Belgrade that was originally run over a hundred years ago. Children also get their own race, a week or two before the main event. ❶ 011 369 0709
Ⓦ www.bgdmarathon.org

May–June

Belgrade Sport Fest Over 100 sporting disciplines in one place plus music and – for the daring – free bungee jumping.
ⓐ Ada Ciganlija ❶ 065 232 5377/063 139 9355 Ⓦ www.belgrade
sportfest.com

June

SVIBOR A rollicking medieval jousting tournament staged by SVIBOR, the Society of Serbian Knightly Fighting, at Kalemegdan. Unfortunately the website does not include an English translation, but the pictures give you some idea of the flavour of the event.
❶ 064 127 1475/064 142 1370 Ⓦ www.svibor.rs

July & August

Belgrade Boat Carnival Plenty of messing about in boats, waterskiing and bridge jumping, topped off by a happy hour and fireworks. ❶ 011 306 1400 Ⓦ www.tob.co.rs

Belgrade Summer Festival (BELEF) This annual festival encompasses a wide array of art performances and activities held across the city, including dance, drama, music and the visual arts (see page 12). ☎ 064 323 8341 or 064 323 8859 🌐 www.belef.org (Serbian)

Belgrade Beer Fest Five days of cheap beer, good music and general revelry. Entrance is free and, thankfully, most people don't come here just to get drunk. ✆ Usce Park, Novi Beograd 🌐 www.belgradebeerfest.com

September

Belgrade International Theatre Festival One of the top European theatre festivals, past BITEF participants include such luminaries as Ingmar Bergman and Steven Berkoff. ✆ 29/1 Terazije (head office) ☎ 011 324 3108 🌐 www.bitef.rs

PUBLIC HOLIDAYS
New Year's Day 1 Jan
Christmas Day 7 Jan
St Sava's Feast Day 27 Jan
National Day of Serbia 15 Feb
Labour Holiday 1 May
Victory Day 9 May
Easter Sunday 15 April 2012, 5 May 2013, 20 April 2014
Vidovdan (Martyrs' Day) 28 June

Note: Serbia follows the Julian calendar, so the dates for Christmas and Easter are not the same as in the UK.

Belgrade Summer Festival (BELEF)

Belgraders love their festivals – and not for them brief one- or two-day affairs. BELEF, the city's summer extravaganza, lasts for a full three weeks in July and August. There are even mini-festivals within the main event. It's an all-encompassing affair that spreads its cultural tentacles around the city. Far from being closeted away in expensive venues for the elite, many of the events are staged in public, and in some of the most popular places, so culture is brought directly to the people. Concerts, films and exhibitions are hosted in Trg Republike and on the streets. The outside of museums might be used as well as the inside. Belgrade's great outdoors is not the only unconventional space involved – you can also go to an art exhibition in a bar. The use of such informal venues reflects the organisers' interactive ethos: public input is encouraged in debates and discussions surrounding the works.

It's impossible to find a theme for BELEF: the philosophy seems to be to put on as wide a range of events as possible so that there's something for everyone. In 2011 there was flamenco, a Green Art market and Green Weekend, and robot theatre. Nor is it an entirely home-grown affair: participants come from the rest of Europe, America and Asia – one year the China Broadcasting Chinese Orchestra gave a performance. The events staged run the gamut from opera, classical music and dance to interactive video and multimedia installations, DJ sessions and rock gigs, and they take place across the city, including at the National Theatre, Terazije Theatre, Madlenianum, Sava Centre, Museum of Contemporary Art, plus various galleries and cultural centres. Consult the festival website for the full programme. Ⓦ www.belef.org (Serbian)

🔺 *Kung-fu fighting at BELEF*

History

Belgrade first crops up in history as a settlement of the Vinca people, a spiritual group fond of their shrines and sacrifices, who ruled the Balkan region and its surroundings about 7,000 years ago. Following their decline, Belgrade had periods under the Celts, Romans and Byzantine Empire, before the Serbs turned up in AD 630. Various groups then vied for control and, after four centuries of squabbling between the Greeks, Hungarians and Bulgarians, the Serbs finally got the upper hand in 1284.

The devastating Battle of Kosovo in 1389 – an early omen of the turmoil the region would suffer right up to modern times – marked the start of the disintegration of the Serbian Empire in the south of the country, but the north, which already had Belgrade as its capital, resisted and prospered, and the city developed fortifications that held off the invading Turks for 70 years. Many such fortifications have survived the centuries and are still largely intact. During the Siege of Belgrade in 1456, the Christian army outwitted the Turks, forcing them to retreat; the victory was credited with saving Christianity.

Eventually, though, the Ottomans gained control of Belgrade in 1521; after a century and a half of peace, it was ruled in turn by the Turks and the Austrians before becoming the capital of the principality of Serbia in 1817. Within a year it had lost its capital status to Kragujevac, but regained it after a few decades, and survived tolerably well, notwithstanding the slow development of the farming-reliant Serbia.

Despite being occupied by both German and Austro-Hungarian forces during World War I, Belgrade developed rapidly as the capital of the newly formed Yugoslav state in the post-war period. But World War II proved more devastating. Despite an attempt to stay out of the hostilities altogether, the city underwent a military coup, invasion by various troops and bombing by both the Germans and the Allies. Thousands died.

Following liberation by the Communists, Belgrade's industrial development continued, and the country largely stayed off the international radar. Then, in 1989, Slobodan Milošević began his 11 years in power. Initially his nationalism proved popular, but within just two years there were street protests against him in Belgrade. But worse was to follow after Milošević's ethnic cleansing in Kosovo led to a NATO bombardment of the capital. In spite of his indictment for war crimes in 1999, the president contested elections in 2000 before finally admitting defeat after massive public protests. He died during his trial in The Hague. Since the end of the Milošević era, Belgrade has endeavoured to leave behind its troubled past and establish itself as a modern and vibrant capital city. The target is now European Union membership: Serbia hopes to open formal negotiations in 2012.

🔵 *Seeing off ancient enemies at Kalemegdan Military Museum*

Lifestyle

Having emerged from past political upheaval and conflict, Belgraders now have an appreciation for quiet recreation. They are a smart and dignified people who go about their business — be it commuting to work, chatting and smoking over a coffee or late-night socialising — calmly and without fuss. Belgrade's citizens are almost universally friendly and welcoming to visitors from outside the country, perhaps helped by the fact that foreign travellers are a relatively new phenomenon.

As is often the case with people who have come through tough times and are not financially well off, Belgrade's citizens are generous friends and hosts. They will be keen to bring out the best they have and to treat you to as much as they can afford. Accept hospitality graciously. Another aspect of life here that you'll have to accept graciously is smoking. The better restaurants usually have non-smoking sections and, generally, more upmarket establishments tend to have stricter controls. However, in bars and cafés any no-smoking signs are regarded as little more than decoration. Cigarettes are not as ubiquitous as they are in some other countries in the region, but Belgrade may still seem smoky to the Western visitor.

Bear in mind that while the city may seem modern and cosmopolitan, Serbia is a conservative and traditional society: open displays of affection between homosexual couples, for example, may not go down well, particularly among older people. Young Belgraders tend to be open-minded, and an impressive number of them speak good English. This is partly due to the popularity of English-language films and TV programmes, including *Only Fools and Horses*, which enjoys a cult following in Serbia.

Visiting Belgrade will generally be reasonably easy on your wallet. The one exception is where accommodation is concerned. Because the tourist industry is still growing, the city has not yet developed the concentration of facilities that results in price-cutting competition, so your hotel may not be as cheap as you'd expect. Anywhere else, be it a restaurant, café, bar, theatre, museum, bus or taxi, the city offers great value.

◆ *A stroll through Trg Studentski Park*

Culture

Given that it has had other priorities in recent years, Belgrade's cultural life is surprisingly developed. While in many former Communist countries the state's suppression of creativity, self-expression and individuality succeeded in quashing the majority's appetite for cultural enrichment, allowing trash culture to take a hold, in Belgrade high culture and the arts have flourished. Whatever your particular interest, you should find something to satisfy it here.

The city has several active cultural centres and institutions; for most of the year they are busy organising festivals showcasing everything from film and music to stunts, beer drinking and jazz. There are fewer events in the winter, though, with the exception of the festivities around Christmas and New Year. But even when no specific event is taking place, there is still a wealth of options for culture vultures. Belgrade's museums cover subjects that run the gamut from African art to Zemun, the far to the near. Contrasts abound: the Banjica Concentration Camp Museum (see page 98), which occupies the site of a former hostage centre and Nazi concentration camp in which thousands of people died, is a few minutes away from the Red Star Belgrade stadium and museum (see pages 93–4), where huge crowds cheer on the city's top team. The Jewish Historical Museum (see page 69) is just around the corner from the city's mosque. Several of the museums host special events and exhibitions, as do the city's many cultural centres, both local and international.

Belgrade has a passion for drama, with the National Theatre (see page 87), which occupies pride of place overlooking the

○ *The National Theatre is Belgrade's oldest and largest*

LISTINGS
Useful English-language publications include *Belgrade Insight* (w http://belgradeinsight.com) and *Belgrade In Your Pocket* (w www.inyourpocket.com), both to be found in tourist information centres and hotels. There is also *Welcome to Belgrade*, the tourist organisation's official guide.

central Trg Republike, complemented by several other venues around the city that stage a mixture of modern and traditional plays, as well as opera and concerts. Unfortunately for visitors, the vast majority of the plays are performed in Serbian, but you may be lucky and find that your visit coincides with an English-language production – check the theatre websites and local press in advance.

There is plenty of classical music and opera on offer, both regular programmes in dedicated venues and one-off events organised by the cultural centres and a couple of museums – again, check the papers. Traditional Serbian and gypsy music and jazz are available more informally in various bars and restaurants.

Belgrade's cultural life is not directed exclusively at adults – its citizens like to develop a thirst for enriching activities in their children from a young age. There are several festivals and events dedicated to children and teenagers, and even a cultural centre that caters solely for them (a Takovska 8 w www.dkcb.rs). Whatever age you are and tastes you have, there will be plenty in Belgrade to sate your cultural appetite.

▶ *Trg Republike blends imposing buildings and open spaces*

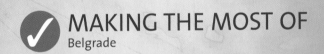

MAKING THE MOST OF
Belgrade

Shopping

Low prices mean that there are bargains aplenty to be had in Belgrade. With the tourist industry still in its infancy, traditional souvenirs are thin on the ground, but leather goods and textiles are cheap and plentiful. Because there is not yet a fully developed tourist market, many of the wares on sale are aimed at the locals; so do some delving – you might find your souvenir between the frying pans and the tomatoes. Shopping in Belgrade is pretty much a no-frills experience, but that is reflected in the prices. There's also a flourishing trade in cheap goods, offering an array of supposedly 'designer' clothes, CDs and DVDs; but these are counterfeit and best avoided.

At the other end of the scale are the genuine designer shops and upmarket boutiques that line Knez Mihailova. Prices are about the same as you'd expect to pay at home, but there are some very good shops to visit here, including a couple of excellent bookshops. With household names such as Hugo Boss, Benetton, Mango and Zara, you could almost think yourself in your local high street. Western-style shopping malls with later opening hours are popular, so if that's what you're after try **Ušće Center** (ⓐ Bulevar Mihajla Pupina 4 ⓦ www.usceshoppingcenter.com), **Delta City** (ⓐ Jurija Gagarina 16, Novi Beograd ⓦ www.deltacity.rs), **City Passage** (ⓐ Obilicev Venac 18–20) or **New Millennium** (ⓐ Knez Mihailova 19–21).

Terazije lies at the heart of Belgrade and is another major shopping area – and a popular meeting place for Belgraders – with shops, department stores and plenty of cafés and restaurants in which to rest your weary feet for a while. Prices drop as you head

◆ *Search for souvenirs amid the fruit stalls*

USEFUL SHOPPING PHRASES

How much is...?
Koliko košta...?
Kolyko koshta...?

Can I try this on?
Mogu li da probam?
Mogoo lee da probam?

I'm a size...
Moja veličina je...
Moya veleecheena ye...

I'll take this one
Uzeću ovu
Oozechoo ovoo

down to Trg Slavija. Also worth a look is Skadarlija (Skadarska), which has a number of interesting little shops, including some attractive art galleries stocking works by local Serbian painters. While you will find many of the big-brand retailers that you'd expect in any major European city, the smaller outlets without famous names – or indeed any name at all – are also worth a look and can often yield surprising bargains.

Street trading makes up much of the commerce. In the centre of Belgrade you will find stalls selling craftwork and women knitting and selling the results of their labours at the same time. The city has some huge markets: these give a real flavour of the Balkan lifestyle, with forthright Serbian and Roma market traders offering all manner of goods. From time to time you might happen upon the occasional fascinating piece of kitschy Communist-era memorabilia. It's always worth haggling if you want to buy something but you feel the price is too high. Be aware, though: the markets are often quite cramped affairs with stalls squeezed together and narrow walkways – take care to protect your valuables.

Eating & drinking

In Serbia, as in much of the Balkans and Eastern Europe, meat is king. Since it is considered a luxury, many people cannot understand why anyone would willingly forgo it. That said, Belgrade is becoming increasingly international, and caters to a wide range of foreign palates, with Italian food particularly prevalent. A few vegetarian options appear on most menus. The standard of food is generally high and you should eat well on your trip, particularly if you are prepared to pay a little more and go to the better eateries. It's worth doing so once or twice, even if you're on a budget, as the highest-quality meal in Belgrade will still be cheap for a Western visitor.

If you really want to experience true Serbian cuisine, hearty meat is the way to go: lamb, veal, beef and pork are popular choices. A typical starter consists of smoked meats, often with a spicy dip. For the main course, the methods of cooking meat are multifarious: it can come roasted, grilled, in a stew, kebab, patty, or as a sausage. Belgrade's history has left its mark on the city's cuisine, which borrows heavily from Turkish cookery. Vegetables feature in salads or combined with meat, such as

PRICE CATEGORIES
Price ratings in this book are based on the average price of a three-course meal without drinks.
£ up to 1,000 dinars **££** 1,000–2,000 dinars
£££ over 2,000 dinars

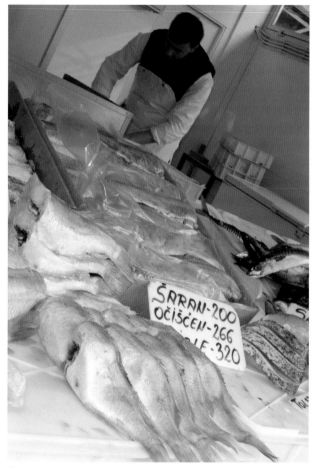

⬥ Catch of the day

peppers, courgettes or cabbage leaves stuffed with meat and rice. Other commonly used vegetables include aubergine and tomato as well as onion (sometimes raw) and garlic. Fish also features, particularly in the riverside restaurants of Novi Beograd, although the distance from the city to the sea pushes the price up somewhat.

On the sweet side, cakes, pastries, pancakes and ice cream of any size and shape are available from cafés as a snack throughout the day; pastries are sometimes also eaten for breakfast and are good on the go. Belgraders often wash down their cake with a coffee, which could be Italian or Turkish style. If you want something stronger, many high-quality Serbian wines, both red and white, are available at very reasonable prices. But the country's flagship alcoholic beverage is its range of challenging spirits, of which *sljivovica*, a plum brandy popular across the region, is perhaps the most famous. It is not for the faint-hearted.

Serbs often take their main meal in the middle of the day, and consume less in the evening. However, the city is now gearing up for its tourists and there's a lively restaurant scene that goes on until 23.00 or 24.00, if not later, so you can normally get what you want when you want. The one exception to that rule is that many cafés do not serve any food at all on Sundays, so do check before you settle down for a meal. Unlike in the UK or US, restaurants, cafés and bars seldom fit strictly into one category – you can often get a snack in a bar or just have a drink in a restaurant. Some eateries' hours change so frequently that it is not worth stating any set times: in this guide, where no hours are given you should phone and check in advance if you'd like to pay a visit.

USEFUL DINING PHRASES

I'd like a table for (two)
Želeo bih sto za (dvoje)
Zheleo beeh sto za (dvoye)

Waiter!
Konobar!
Konobar!

Does it have meat in it?
Da li je sa mesom?
Da lee ye sa mesom?

Could I have the bill please?
Molim vas račun?
Moleem vas rachoon?

Excuse me, where are the toilets?
Izvinite, gde je toalet?
Izveeneete, gde ye towalet?

If you dine out with locals, don't attempt to split the bill – covering the cost is the host's responsibility and, as a foreigner, the host is unlikely to be you, regardless of any intention you might have to pay. The concept of leaving a 10 or 15 per cent tip in a restaurant is not considered mandatory in Belgrade, but it is appreciated if you round up the bill.

Belgrade is full of great parks for alfresco dining, with Ada Ciganlija a particularly popular spot. Pick up your cake and pastries from a bakery; you should be able to get the rest of your provisions from markets or small supermarkets.

Entertainment & nightlife

Belgraders have a big appetite for fun, which is manifested in their city's nightlife. In the 1990s, after the fall of Communism, techno music caught on in a big way, as did turbo-folk, an all-too-catchy combination of traditional Serbian song, electronic beats and Oriental influences (see page 107). Today there is a raft of good dance clubs, and raft is perhaps an appropriate term: many of the city's nightspots are housed in boats floating on the river – called *splavovi* – which bang out their rhythms into the early hours. These venues are frequented by Belgrade's new money, out to parade its wealth. The calibre of the clientele is not always of the highest; that said, they are still worth a visit to see the flashier side of Belgrade's post-Communist culture. Other clubs are housed in small basement settings, and these tend to be less pretentious.

The club scene has attracted top international DJs, and Belgrade's style-conscious party people dress for the occasion, so if you go out to certain venues in casual gear, you may feel underdressed. Things do not get started until late – don't expect to see much action in the city's clubs before midnight – and if you want to party like a real Belgrader you should still be going when the sun comes up.

But not all nightlife is of the frenetic kind. Cafés and bars often keep late hours and it's not unusual to see people strolling around Knez Mihailova or sitting with a coffee and a cake well after midnight. There is often entertainment in public spaces, with concerts frequently staged in Trg Republike and festivals such as Open Heart Day and BELEF that include street theatre.

○ Catch a concert in Trg Republike

Check the tourist information website (see page 135) and the English-language listings guides mentioned on page 20 for upcoming events.

Although most of the plays staged in the capital are in Serbian, you will find the odd one in English. Most of the city's main venues keep updated websites that list what's on and flag up any English-language shows. You can sometimes order tickets online; otherwise the box offices are normally open quite extensive hours. Don't pay too much attention to whether a venue is described as a theatre, opera house or so on: most of the top establishments host productions from across the board – drama, music, ballet and sometimes art. Like much in the city, cultural pursuits will not dent the budget: a ticket to one of the top concert venues or theatres will set you back no more than 800 dinars.

While you might not be lucky enough to catch a play that you can understand during your trip, cinemas do tend to cater to English-speakers – films are shown in their original language, not dubbed, which means a range of American movies is on offer. If you fancy seeing something other than the usual blockbusters, the Muzej Kinoteke broadcasts classic films. In summer several venues hold open-air screenings.

Upwards of a dozen concerts take place every week in Belgrade. Listings can be found on the Tourist Organisation of Belgrade website, along with pertinent information such as venues, dates, ticket prices and where to get tickets (which is now possible online).

Sport & relaxation

If you fancy some sport, your best bet is to cross the water to Ada Ciganlija island. As well as the more hair-raising extreme and water sports, such as bungee jumping, kayaking and paintball, there's also a range of less terrifying pastimes, including tennis, volleyball, five-a-side football, roller-skating, basketball, baseball, rowing and rugby. The island also hosts Serbia's first-ever golf course. Even chess is available, if you like your sports and games to involve minimum physical exertion. A word of warning: in summer, the island can get crowded.

Hala Sportova (Sports Hall 🔵 Pariske komune 20 🕿 011 267 1547) in Novi Beograd can pack in up to 5,000 fans for the sports events it hosts, including basketball, handball, boxing and various martial arts. Hala Pionir in Tašmajdan is a similar indoor spectator sport arena, and the park has another sports centre with swimming facilities. There are several other sports complexes in the city; check with the tourist information office (see page 135) for current details.

If you've heard about Belgrade in a sporting context, however, it's likely to have been because of the country's top football club, Red Star Belgrade, and its bitter rival FK Partizan. Their enmity is bound up with the story of the city and its troubles – Red Star fan and alleged war criminal Arkan recruited for his paramilitary organisation from among the ranks of the city's football hooligans. The club is also a part of wider football history: they were Manchester United's opposition in 1958 before the Munich air disaster, in which eight United players died when their plane crashed after take-off on the way home. Today matches in

Belgrade are usually quieter than in the past, when violent flare-ups were fairly common. Despite both clubs modernising, neither offers anything like an online booking system – it's best just to go to the ground. Both clubs have teams in several sports other than football, so there are plenty of opportunities to experience the passionate Red Star–Partizan rivalry, whatever your sporting proclivities. See page 94 for contact details and opening times.

Red Star's 'Maracana' stadium has a capacity of more than 50,000

Accommodation

While entertainment, eating and transport options in Belgrade are all plentiful and good value, the city is lagging behind in terms of accommodation. Emerging from Communism takes time, and many hotels are still run by the state. And it shows — in stiff service, drab rooms and lobbies whose cheap-looking décor could date from the 1970s. Given that Belgrade is generally inexpensive by capital city standards, prices for accommodation are higher than you'd imagine. There are some excellent hotels, but they are aimed at the business traveller rather than the tourist and are likely to be beyond the budget of many visitors. What's more, the best hotels are mostly on the Novi Beograd side of the river, which will put you some distance from the main sites. Unless you don't mind making your way back and forth over the bridge every day, it's better to base yourself nearer the centre. (If you have a car, don't mind using it and really want value for money from your accommodation, a night in a five-star hotel in Novi Sad can be cheaper than a dingy two- or three-star place in the capital.)

PRICE CATEGORIES
The following categories are based on the average price for a double room per night.
£ up to 7,000 dinars   ££ 7,000–12,000 dinars
£££ over 12,000 dinars

It's not all bad news. Hotels are rapidly being privatised, renovated and upgraded, and new ones are opening up both inside and outside the city centre. This is helping to raise standards and cut prices (which, incidentally, are sometimes quoted in euros as well as in dinars). One option is to look for short-term accommodation, i.e. find a rental apartment over the Internet.

Cheap hotels are concentrated around the station. The area is not great, but the accommodation is not as bad as you sometimes

◔ *The Balkan hotel enjoys a very central position*

find around stations. Hostels have proliferated in recent years, catering to the off-the-beaten-track backpacking crowd.

You can usually turn up on spec and find a room in your price range, but it cannot be guaranteed – and during some of the more popular festivals, the cheaper rooms can be booked solid, so it's worth planning ahead if you don't want to end up pounding Belgrade's pavements with your luggage. Fortunately, it's easy to book in advance: you can either contact your preferred hotel directly, or book online through one of several organisations. Try the National Tourist Organisation of Serbia or the Tourist Organisation of Belgrade (see page 135), or **Visit Serbia** (ⓦ www.visitserbia.org). Where no public transport options are listed for the following hotels, the only way to reach them is on foot or by taxi.

HOTELS
Royal Hotel £ Consistently rated one of the best hotels in its price bracket, your buck gets you a cooked breakfast and a little bit of history – the Royal is the oldest hotel in Belgrade. There's an internet café on site as well as free Wi-Fi. ⓐ Kralja Petra 56 (Kalemegdan Fortress & around) ⓣ 011 263 4222 ⓦ www.hotelroyal.rs

Slavija Lux £–££ The Slavija Lux offers clean rooms in a central location, while its adjacent sister hotel is a budget option. ⓐ Svetog Save 2 ⓣ 011 244 1120 ⓦ www.slavijahotel.com

Kasina ££ Beer aficionados will like Kasina, which boasts its own brewery. It's central and has a few more modern

○ *The landmark Moskva hotel*

rooms as well as a decent café, where you can sit outside.
🅐 Terazije 25 (Trg Republike & city centre) ☎ 011 323 5574
Ⓦ www.kasina-belgrade.hotel-rn.com Ⓝ Trolleybus: 19, 21, 22, 29; bus: 31

Hotel Union ££ The décor may have seen better days, but the central location and friendly staff are compensations, and visitors weaned on bland chain hotels may even enjoy the Soviet chic. Dedicated parking spaces right outside are another plus.
🅐 Kosovska 11 (Trg Republike) ☎ 011 324 8022 Ⓦ www.hotelunion belgrade.com

Excelsior ££–£££ A major overhaul under new management has reinvigorated the Excelsior, which now provides tasteful, modern four-star accommodation in harmony with the style of the historic building. The on-site nightclub has also thankfully gone. The park views are another plus, as are the helpful staff.
🅐 Kneza Miloša 5 (Trg Republike & city centre) ☎ 011 323 1381
Ⓦ www.hotelexcelsior.co.rs Ⓝ Bus: 23, 37, 44, 58

Balkan £££ Renovated and upgraded a few years ago, this hotel offers comfortable rooms and a dead-central location. It's quieter than you might expect given its setting, and the upper floors offer good views of the city. 🅐 Prizrenska 2 (Trg Republike & city centre) ☎ 011 363 6000 Ⓦ www.balkanhotel.net
Ⓝ Trolleybus: 19, 21, 22, 29; bus: 31

Hotel Square Nine £££ Ultra-stylish and sumptuously comfortable, this brand-new facility is already making waves on the award scene. Rooms are done out with class and flair, and the service is exemplary. Square Nine also enjoys the best location of Belgrade's high-end hotels, and a roof bar is being opened to better exploit the city view. ⓐ Trg Studentski 9 ☏ 011 333 3500 ⓦ www.squarenine.rs

Moskva £££ One of the city's most famous landmarks, this Art Nouveau building is now over a hundred years old, and history seeps through it. The rooms have character and class. ⓐ Balkanska 1 (Trg Republike & city centre) ☏ 011 268 6255 ⓦ www.hotelmoskva.rs ⓝ Trolleybus: 19, 21, 22, 29; bus: 31

Le Petit Piaf £££ Small but superior hotel that punches above its 3-star category. Rooms are bright, airy and tasteful. ⓐ Skadarska 34 (Trg Republike & city centre) ☏ 011 303 5252 ⓦ www.petit piaf.com

HOSTELS
Hostel Belgrade £ Just off Knez Mihailova, this small but very welcoming hostel has bright, lively staff who are happy to share a beer or two with guests when they get in from the pub. ⓐ Kralja Milana 17 (Trg Republike & city centre) ☏ 063 723 8130 ⓦ www.hostelbelgrade.com ⓝ Bus: 23, 37, 44, 58

Three Black Catz £ Small, central and friendly, this is one of the most alternative places to hang out in Belgrade. Although cats are no longer in residence, there's still a cat theme throughout the ten-room hostel. ⓐ Cika Ljubica 7/49 (Trg Republike & city centre) ☏ 011 262 9826 ⓦ www.hostel.co.rs

THE BEST OF BELGRADE

There's plenty to enjoy in Belgrade, but these are the sights that should really not be missed.

TOP 10 ATTRACTIONS

- **Kalemegdan** Combining history, green space and a laid-back vibe, Kalemegdan Park and Fortress encapsulate three of the best things about modern Belgrade (see pages 62 & 64).

- **Princess Ljubica's Konak** Built by Prince Obrenović for his wife Ljubica, this is a superb example of 19th-century Serbian architecture (see pages 65 & 67).

- **Skadarlija** The bohemian style of Skadarlija's early Roma settlers is clear in the city's cobbled restaurant district (see pages 80–81).

- **Federal Parliament building** Both a stunning structure and the symbolic place where Milošević was forced out of Serbian politics (see pages 77 & 80).

❥ *Belgrade's pedestrian-friendly centre is ripe for exploration*

- **Riverside fish restaurants** With a bewildering array of sea creatures from which to choose, Novi Beograd's floating eateries are well worth a visit (see pages 111–12).

- **A Red Star Belgrade match** With 50,000 Serbs passionately cheering on their team, watching a match at the so-called Serbian 'Maracana' stadium is a great experience (see pages 32–3 & 93–4).

- **Floating nightclubs** Belgrade's chic set get dressed up and hit the riverboat clubs, ready for a night of catchy Serbian turbo-folk (see page 108).

- **Tito Memorial Complex** The fascinating collection of diplomatic gifts that Tito amassed during his time as Yugoslav leader shows why a statesman never has to worry about home décor (see pages 92–3).

- **River cruises** If the city's complex network of one-way systems is pushing up your blood pressure, abandon the road and take to the water (see page 109).

- **St Sava's Church** Well over 100 years from conception, it's still not finished, but the church is imposing from afar and magnificent close up (see pages 95–7).

Suggested itineraries

HALF-DAY: BELGRADE IN A HURRY

Start with a walk along Knez Mihailova. Unless the weather is terrible you should stroll around Kalemegdan and take some panoramic shots of the town. It's a short walk from here to the Orthodox Cathedral and Princess Ljubica's Konak. If it really is too cold or wet for the park (provided it's not Monday), the Ethnographic Museum and Military Museum are nearby and doable in less than an hour. If you're having dinner, head to Skadarlija.

1 DAY: TIME TO SEE A LITTLE MORE

In a day you can do all of the above, and have time to see something outside the Old Town. That could be the impressive St Sava's Church or, if you prefer to pack more in, you could go to the much nearer Federal Parliament building, which is opposite St Mark's Church and Tašmajdan Park. If you have the energy, round the day off with a visit to one of the basement bars in the centre of town.

2–3 DAYS: TIME TO SEE MUCH MORE

Your next priority should be the Tito Memorial Complex. It's quite a trek but it takes you near to the Red Star and Partizan football stadiums, where you may be able to catch a game or check out the Red Star museum, and the street of embassies. You can also head over the river to take in Novi Beograd's Museum of Contemporary Art, restaurants and nightlife and enjoy a concert or show.

LONGER: ENJOYING BELGRADE TO THE FULL

Now you can factor in the markets, parks and smaller museums that give a more authentic taste of Belgrade, and relax a while at Kalemegdan or Ada Ciganlija. You can also see something else of Serbia: its second city Novi Sad can be done in a day, or you could overnight there and explore more of the area, including the beautiful monasteries of Fruška Gora National Park (see Out of Town Trips, pages 116–17).

● *Begin your tour with a stroll along Knez Mihailova*

Something for nothing

Belgrade is a city that's perfect to walk around, and it's quite possible to have a fulfilling day or two without spending very much at all. Many of the city's main attractions are outside and, provided the weather is fine, you can easily take in the atmosphere by strolling around pedestrianised streets such as Knez Mihailova and Skadarska, and doing a spot of window-shopping or people-watching. There are also several parks and public spaces where you can spend a pleasant few hours. Kalemegdan (see pages 62 & 64) costs nothing unless you want to go up its clock tower, and Ada Ciganlija island (see pages 32, 88 & 92), Tašmajdan Park (see page 97) and Hajd Park – further south on the way to the Tito Memorial Complex and the football stadiums – will also leave the wallet untroubled. A wander along the riverside is another enticing option on a sunny day.

The odd museum, such as the Fresco Gallery (see page 69), has free entrance. Several of the paying attractions also offer free days and weekends, but there seems to be no hard-and-fast rule about when these are: if you're on a budget and have the time to do the research, it's worth asking ahead or checking the relevant website. Some of the most important sites in the capital are its religious buildings, St Sava's (see pages 95–7) and the Cathedral (see page 67) among them, for which there is no entrance fee. The ornate Cathedral is fascinating, while the monumental St Sava's is also surrounded by charming gardens, from which there are superb views.

Nor will you have to dig deep in your pocket to experience Belgrade's cultural life: the Serbian Academy of Sciences & Arts (see page 75) hosts free classical concerts on Monday and Thursday at 18.00 from the beginning of October to the end of June, and you will find other concerts and shows for which entrance is free. The city's cultural institutions take an inclusive attitude to their events, and many of the festivals offer free admission, public performances and street theatre.

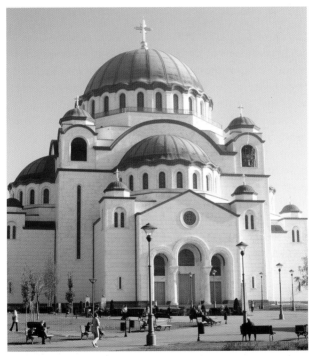

⬤ *Feast your eyes for free at St Sava's*

When it rains

Belgrade can get quite a lot of rain in the spring months and can be very chilly in winter, so it's a good idea to have a few indoor places in mind to visit if you're travelling at those times. Although many of its tourist sites are in the open air, the city also has a wealth of museums, galleries, churches and cultural centres that are enjoyable whatever the weather.

One place that it's worth making a special visit to on a wet day is the Museum of Yugoslav Cinema (see pages 82–3), which broadcasts titles from the extensive national archive, 80 per cent of which are foreign. Watching a film here is an enjoyable experience, and the range of pictures screened is ambitious.

If shopping is more your thing, you needn't be thwarted by a downpour. The markets or window-shopping on Knez Mihailova might not appeal if the weather is miserable, but the centre of the city has a few malls that you can potter around in perfect warmth and comfort (see page 22). Some of the large halls at Belgrade Fair (see pages 98–9) have also been given over to a permanent bazaar selling a motley collection of useful items – as an added advantage it's open on Sundays.

Another option of course is to dry off and warm up in one of the many cafés, bars, restaurants or combinations thereof. Many of them offer customers a selection of newspapers and magazines, or you can just relax, sit back and watch Belgrade go by. Wet weather provides a perfect excuse to head for one of the posh hotels – their drinks and snacks may be verging on the extortionate by Serbian standards, but almost everyone except those travelling on the shortest of shoestrings will be able to stretch to a tea or coffee – and maybe lunch if the weather doesn't perk up.

⏷ *Escape showers at the Tito Memorial Complex*

On arrival

TIME DIFFERENCE

Serbia follows Central European Time. During Daylight Saving Time (end Mar–end Oct), the clocks are put ahead by one hour.

ARRIVING

By air

The majority of visitors fly into Terminal 2 of Belgrade's Nikola Tesla, better known as Surčin Airport (ⓦ www.beg.aero), which is 18 km (11 miles) west of the city centre. Formerly somewhat grim, it has been modernised, and now has a decent selection of shops and amenities. There's an ATM and you can exchange your foreign currency; the rates are usually comparable with what you would find in the city centre.

The A1 shuttle bus runs around the clock between the airport and Trg Slavija. It departs as frequently as every 20 minutes during busy times, but you might have to wait an hour or longer in the wee hours. The fare, one way, is around 250 dinars; pay the driver directly. The number 72 public bus leaves the airport half-hourly, making several stops before terminating at Zeleni Venac, a large bus terminal not far from Trg Republike. It takes about ten minutes longer than the A1 bus, but costs under half the price – even less if you buy your ticket in advance from a newspaper kiosk.

By Western standards, a taxi from the airport into town is not expensive – official taxis have a flat rate and you shouldn't pay much more than 1,500 dinars; rates go up at weekends and on public holidays. However, rip-off merchants hang around waiting to target tourists, with many posing as licensed taxi drivers, complete with official-looking badge. To avoid being fleeced, ignore all offers of a taxi from individuals in the arrivals hall and either walk to the Terminal 1 departures hall and hail one of the cabs dropping people off, or pre-book a taxi from a reputable company – some offer a 20 per cent discount on pre-booked fares. To call a taxi yourself dial ❶ 970 (❶ 011 970 if you're using a mobile) or go to the official tourist office at the airport, where they will call one for you. It's also now possible to text a taxi – send a message reading: T Medjunarodni Dolasci Aerodrom to ❶ 649700. They will send you a message back with the number of the car that will come for you and how many minutes until it arrives. The journey takes around 15–20 minutes.

◆ *The Danube is useful for orientation*

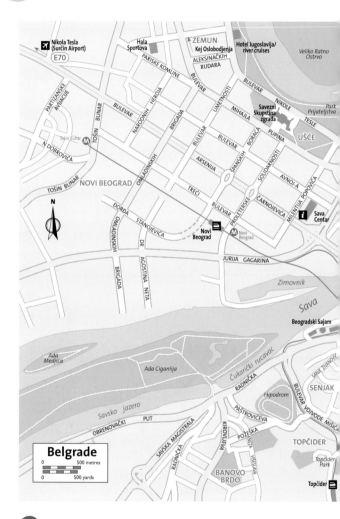

Belgrade

0   500 metres
0   500 yards

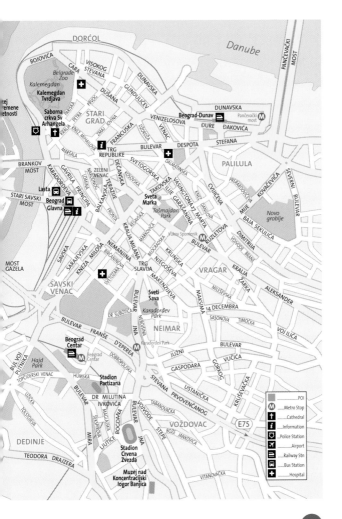

DORĆOL

Danube

PANČEVAČKI MOST

BOJOVIĆA

VISOKOG
STEVANA

CARA
DUŠANA

DUNAVSKA

GUNDULIĆEV

Belgrade
Zoo

Kalemegdan
Tvrdjava

zej
emene
etnosti

Saborna
crkva Sv
Arhangela

STARI
GRAD

PETRA

PILOG

KRALJA

CARA

DUŠANA

DUNAVSKA

Beograd-Dunav

Pančevački
most

VENIZELOSOVA

ĐURE ĐAKOVIĆA

PALILULA

KNEZ MIHAILOVA

MARŠALA

FRANCUSKA

DŽORDŽA

STEFANA

DESPOTA

DALMATINSKA

BRANKOV
MOST

TRG
REPUBLIKE

KARAĐORĐEVA

GAVRILA PRINCIPA

ZELENI
VENAC

DEČANSKA

SVETOGORSKA

CVIJIĆEVA

PREPARODNA

MIJE KOVAČEVIĆA

SEVERNI BULEVAR

STARI SAVSKI
MOST

Lasta

Beograd
Glavna

BALKANSKA

TERAZIJE

NUŠIĆEVA

TAKOVSKA

ILIJE GARAŠANINA

VAŠINGTONA

27 MARTA

KNEZ DANILOVA

Novo
groblje

BAJA SEKULIĆA

MOST
GAZELA

SAVSKA

SARAJEVSKA

KNEZA MILOŠA

NEMANJINA

BIRČANINOVA

KRALJA MILANA

FRONTA

RESAVSKA

BEOGRADSKA

MARKOVIĆA

Sveta
Marka

Tašmajdan
Park

Vukov Spomenik

KURSULINA

KRUNSKA

BULEVAR

DIMITRIJA

VOJVODE BRANE

VRAGAR

KRALJA

ŽARKA

ALEKSANDER

SAVSKI
VENAC

SVETOZARA

BULEVAR

NJEGOŠEVA

TRG
SLAVIJA

MAKENZIJEVA

Sveti
Sava

Karađorđev
Park

MAKSIMA

14 DECEMBRA

MILEŠEVSKA

SAŠONOVA

TIMOČKA

VOJ ILIĆA

DR SUBOTIĆA

NEBOJŠINA

INA

NEIMAR

BULEVAR

FRANŠE

D'EPEREA

DOBROPOLJSKA

Karađorđev Park

JUŽNI

GASPODAR

BULEVAR

VUČIĆA

ĆORĆOG

KRUŠEVAČKA

Beograd
Centar

Beograd
Centar

BUL VOJ
PUTNIKA

Hajd
Park

TOPČIDERSKI VENAC

HUMSKA

Stadion
Partizana

BULEVAR

DR MILUTINA
IVKOVIĆA

NAHLASKA

SKOPANSKA

BOGDANA

STEVANA PRVOVENČANOG

USTANIČKA

TABANOVAČKA

VOJVODE

BULEVAR

VITANOVAČKA

E75

UŽIČKA

TOLSTOJEVA

DEDINJE

TEODORA DRAJZERA

MIRA

LJUTICE

INA

VOŽDOVAC

STEPE

BOŽE JANKOVIĆA

Stadion
Crvena
Zvezda

Muzej nad
Koncentracijski
logor Banjica

	POI
M	Metro Stop
✝	Cathedral
i	Information
🛡	Police Station
✈	Airport
🚆	Railway Stn
🚌	Bus Station
✚	Hospital

IF YOU GET LOST, TRY ...

Do you speak English?
Da li pričate engleski?
Dah-lee preechate enghleski?

Is this the way to...?
Da li je ovo put do...?
Da lee ye ovo poot do...?

Could you point it out on the map?
Pokazite mi na mapi?
Pokazheete mee na mapee?

By rail
Train travel in Serbia is not the height of luxury – nor is Beograd Centar, the station in Belgrade – but, on the plus side, trains to Belgrade do bring you very close to the city centre, which is just a short walk up the hill to the left as you come out.

By road
You're likely to enter Belgrade on the E70 or E75. From the highway follow signs to the centre (*centar*), and from there look – hard – for the small signs to the major squares and landmarks. The city has a slightly strange pavement parking system (ⓦ www.parking-servis.co.rs), with zones categorised red, yellow and green, where you are permitted to park for one, two or three hours at a staggered hourly rate. Payment is by a ticket bought at a kiosk by SMS or from a machine (in the red zone). There are occasional one-way systems that are quite complicated to navigate.

The bus station is right next door to the central train station. In fact, various buses, trolleybuses and trams pass by the station or very close to it. If you do need to take a taxi somewhere, avoid the ones parked outside the station, which will probably rip you off, and hail one from further away.

FINDING YOUR FEET

Belgrade is not so different from other European capitals, apart from the occasional bomb-damaged building, and you are unlikely to suffer culture shock. As in any large city, there is crime, and foreigners can be appealing targets, especially for pickpockets. Keep your wits about you in the bus and train stations, at markets and in all crowded places.

ORIENTATION

Belgrade's centre point is effectively Trg Republike, which is the mid-point on the city's central street – the pedestrianised Knez Mihailova going northwest and Terazije, later becoming Kralja Milana, in the opposite direction. Kalemegdan Fortress to the north and St Sava's Church to the south both tower above the city and serve as useful orientation points. The rivers Sava and Danube are also helpful indicators.

GETTING AROUND

The city has an integrated and comprehensive public transport system of buses, trolleybuses (except in Novi Beograd) and trams. Tickets cost around 100 dinars if you pay on board, and half that if you buy them in advance from a kiosk. Fares are slightly higher if you're travelling between 24.00 and 04.00. Make sure you

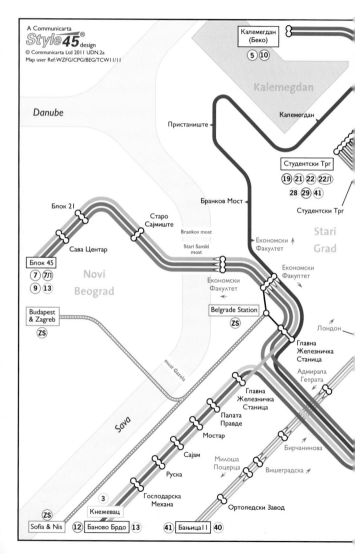

A Communicarta
Style45 design
© Communicarta Ltd 2011 | UDN.2a
Map user Ref:WZFG/CPG/BEG/TCW11/11

Калемегдан
(Беко)
(5) (10)

Kalemegdan

Danube

Калемегдан

Пристаниште

Студентски Трг
(19) (21) (22) (22Л)
(28) (29) (41)

Студентски Трг

Бранков Мост

Блок 21

Старо
Сајмиште

Brankov most

Економски
Факултет

Stari
Grad

Сава Центар

Stari Savski
most

Економски
Факултет

Блок 45
(7) (7Л)
(9) (13)

Novi
Beograd

Економски
Факултет

Belgrade Station
(ZS)

Лондон

Budapest
& Zagreb
(ZS)

Главна
Железничка
Станица

Админрала
Гепрата

most Gazela

Главна
Железничка
Станица

Sava

Палата
Правде

Мостар

Бирчанинова

Сајам

Милоша
Поцерца

Вишеградска

Руска

(3)

Господарска
Механа

Кнежевац

Ортопедски Завод

(ZS)
Sofia & Nis

(12) Баново Брдо (13)

(41) Бањица11 (40)

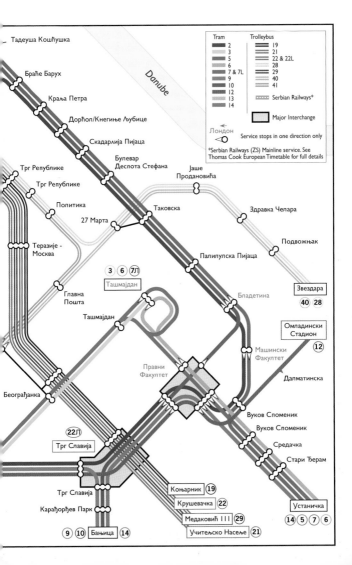

Тадеуша Кошћушка

Danube

Браће Барух

Краља Петра

Дорћол/Кнегиње Љубице

Скадарлија Пијаца

Булевар
Деспота Стефана

Јаше
Продановића

Трг Републике

Трг Републике

Политика

Таковска

Здравка Челара

27 Марта

Подвожњак

Теразије -
Москва

Палилулска Пијаца

Лондон

Service stops in one direction only

*Serbian Railways (ZS) Mainline service. See
Thomas Cook European Timetable for full details

Tram
2
3
5
6
7 & 7L
9
10
12
13
14

Trolleybus
19
21
22 & 22L
28
29
40
41

Serbian Railways*

Major Interchange

③ ⑥ ⑦Л
Ташмајдан

Бладетина

Звездара
⑩ ㉘

Главна
Пошта

Ташмајдан

Омладински
Стадион
⑫

Правни
Факултет

Машински
Факултет

Далматинска

Београђанка

Вуков Споменик

Вуков Споменик

㉒Л

Средачка

Трг Славија

Стари Ђерам

Трг Славија

Коњарник ⑲

Карађорђев Парк

Крушевачка ㉒

Медаковић III ㉙

Устаничка

⑨ ⑩ Бањица ⑭

Учитељско Насеље ㉑

⑭⑤⑦⑥

punch your ticket once on board or it won't be valid. There is also a limited metro service. Things can get pretty packed during rush hour. Major transport hubs are at Trg Republike and Trg Slavija. The transport system has a useful website with more information (ⓦ www.gsp.rs). Public buses also go to Novi Sad, as do trains: it lies on the Belgrade–Budapest route. For train information see the English-language **Serbian railways** website at ⓦ www.serbianrailways.com

For travel within the city, taxis are cheap. The majority of drivers – airport and station touts excepted – are honest, and the fare for a short ride in the centre should not exceed 400 or 500 dinars. Check the taxi has a sticker indicating the charges and a working meter. The meter begins running at around 140 dinars.

Car hire

While a car is useful for nipping back and forth across the river, or for journeys further afield such as to Novi Sad, Belgrade is small enough, the transport system comprehensive enough and taxis cheap enough that it is not a necessity in the city. If you do hire a car, expect to pay the equivalent of £100 for three days.

Avis ⓐ Hotel Hyatt Regency, Milentija Popovica 5 ⓣ 011 313 9616 ⓦ www.avis.rs

Budget ⓐ Belgrade Airport ⓣ 011 228 6361 ⓦ www.budget.co.uk

Hertz ⓐ Hotel Putnik, Dragoslava Jovanovica 1 ⓣ 011 320 8736 ⓦ www.hertz.co.uk

---

Ⓞ *Looking across the city from Kalemegdan Fortress*

THE CITY OF
Belgrade

Kalemegdan Fortress & around

Perfectly encapsulating Belgrade's reconciliation of its bloody history with its laid-back present is Kalemegdan Fortress, the city's flagship site of historical interest. The fortress itself, some 2,000 years old, sits in the middle of a vast park beloved of Belgraders. The main entrance to the park leads directly on to the pedestrian zone centred around Knez Mihailova. Despite its Roman origins, the street is thoroughly modern in atmosphere, with a cluster of designer stores and lots of places for eating, drinking and shopping that are open late into the night. The area is also home to much of the city's cultural life, with various museums, galleries, monuments and places of worship dotted around, including, near the southernmost tip of the park, the Orthodox Cathedral and, diagonally across from it, Princess Ljubica's Konak.

The area is entirely pedestrianised and there is no public transport; prepare to do some serious walking if you want to explore the park and fortress, which cover more than 20 hectares (50 acres). It's well worth the effort, though, as the uppermost part gives you some of the best views of the meeting point of the Danube and Sava rivers. The rest of the Old Town is bisected by Knez Mihailova, and if you get lost you can usually get your bearings again by identifying that.

SIGHTS & ATTRACTIONS

Bajrakli Dzamija (Bajrakli Mosque)

Belgrade's only mosque has survived conversion to a church, abandonment by the Turks and fire damage during riots in its

◔ *Bajrakli Mosque*

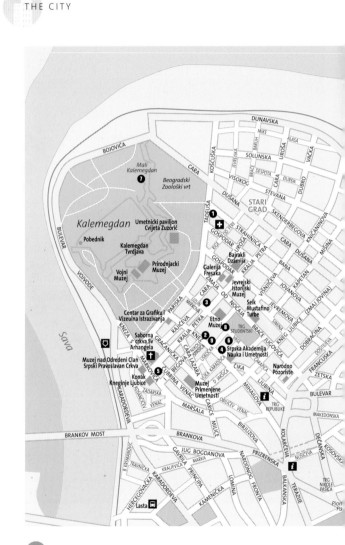

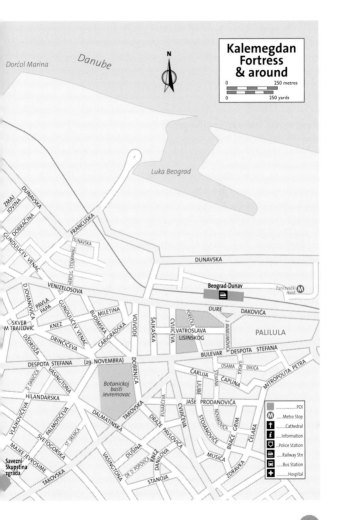

Dorćol Marina

Danube

N

Kalemegdan Fortress & around

0 — 250 metres
0 — 250 yards

Luka Beograd

ZMAJ JOVINA
DUNAVSKA
DOBRAĆINA
GUNDULIĆEV VENAC
FRANCUSKA
DUNAVSKA

KNEZ MIHAILA STEPANU

DUNAVSKA

Beograd-Dunav

Pančevački most (M)

VENIZELOSOVA

D JOVANOVIĆA
PAVLA PAPA
GUNDULIĆEV VENAC
MILETINA
BUDIMSKA
VOJVODE
SAJKAŠKA
CVIKEVA
PORECA
MAKIMOVICA
DURE
DAKOVIĆA

SKVER M TRAILOVIĆ
KNEZ
CARIGRADSKA

PALILULA

DŽORDŽA
DRINČIĆEVA
VATROSLAVA LISINSKOG

DESPOTA STEFANA
(29. NOVEMBRA)
DOBRNICA
BULEVAR DESPOTA STEFANA

D DANIČLA
VAŠINGTONA
Botanickoj basti Jevremovac
OSAMA
STOJAN
ČAPLINA
DIKIĆA
MITROPOLITA PETRA

ČARLIJA

HILANDARSKA
LJUBE
RUVARCIJA
JAŠE PRODANOVIĆA

VIJAKOVIĆEVA
PALMOTIĆEVA
ST SREMCA
DALMATINSKA
TAKOVSKA
DRAŽE PAVLOVIĆA
CVIJKEVA
STOJANOVIĆE
NOVAKOVIĆA
BIJAĆE GRIM
CELARA

SVETOGORSKA
MAJKE JEVROSIME
VAŠINGTONA
DUŠINA
DR D POPOVIĆA
KNEZ DANILOVA
MUSIĆA
ZDRAVKA

Savezni Skupstina zgrada
TAKOVSKA
STANOJA

Legend

POI
(M) Metro Stop
Cathedral
i Information
Police Station
Railway Stn
Bus Station
Hospital

300-plus-year history. Today it's a relatively simple place of worship, particularly compared to the showiness of some of the city's other holy sites, with a replacement minaret, stone walls and a few pictures. ⓐ Gospodar Jevremova 11 ⓣ 011 262 2428 ⓛ 07.00–19.00

Beogradski Zoološki vrt (Belgrade Zoo)

When Nazi bombs hit the zoo in 1941, some of the residents seized their opportunity and made a bold bid for freedom, heading off to explore the war-ravaged town. Today, fortunately, the 2,000 animals from 270 different species are penned in more securely. There's also a café and gift shop. ⓐ Mali Kalemegdan 8 ⓣ 011 262 4526 ⓦ www.beozoovrt.izlog.org ⓛ 08.00–17.00 (winter); 08.00–19.30 (summer) ❶ Admission charge

Kalemegdan Tvrdjava (Kalemegdan Fortress)

Kalemegdan pretty much ticks all the tourist boxes: it's got history dating back to ancient times, it offers one of the best views of the Danube and Sava, and it's also a pleasant place to stroll, read or play, depending on your age and inclination. Throw in a couple of museums and a zoo, and it's easy to see why Belgraders are so fond of it. The fortress is far more than a few old ruins: much of it is extremely well preserved and conveys a real sense of history. Turrets, towers and ramparts are still in fine condition. This atmosphere makes it the ideal home for the city's Military Museum, and the park also hosts the Cvijeta Zuzorić Art Pavilion and the Natural History Museum Gallery (see page 70). Further culture comes in the form of various statues around the grounds, from Pobednik (the Messenger of Victory monument),

◎ *The Messenger of Victory monument towers above the city*

which proudly stands sentinel from a tall plinth, to the same sculptor's Monument to France, and many more.

If you don't fancy looking round museums or studying statues, the park is also great for slow-paced recreation. There are numerous benches for leisurely contemplation of your surroundings, and the stunning views over the meeting point of the Sava and Danube rivers are also worth the effort. The park's main walkway is also home to a hotchpotch market, where you can pick up lace and knitwear, hip flasks, wooden pipes and cigarette lighters (for the less health-conscious) and even Communist-era memorabilia. Children are particularly well catered for, with various amusements including a zoo, mini funfair and balloon sellers. They also seem to love clambering all over the complex's replica tanks and guns, which re-create European and American weapons from the last century or so. Most of the complex is open for general wandering and exploration, but be warned – there are almost no signs and it is very easy to get lost, which, given the size of the place, can be tiring and tiresome. If you wish to take a more structured approach, audio guides to the site can be rented from various kiosks and information points in the park.

Aside from the museums, it's also worth making a point of visiting the clock tower. As well as climbing to the top, you can also view a selection of photos, a model of the fort and a historical display covering the site's various phases under Roman, Austrian and Turkish influence. A helpful guide is on hand to answer any questions. ⓦ www.beogradska tvrdjava.co.rs ⓒ Clock tower: 10.00–17.00 ⓥ Tram: 2, 5, 10, 11, 13 ⓘ Admission charge for tower

Knez Mihailova

The pedestrianised area around Knez Mihailova (the street running northwest from Trg Republike, also known as Kneza Mihaila) is the city's beating heart, reflecting the many phases and faces of Belgrade. During the day it's a bustling shopping district, full of Belgraders seeking fashion and food. At night it's a buzzing party place, brimming with excited, dolled-up teenagers on their way to a night of revelry. On Sundays and in the lulls between action it's calm and quiet, as the townsfolk chat over coffee or stroll and gossip.

Despite having its origins in Roman times, the area feels so modern and Western that, as you glance around and take in the perfectly flat paved surface and the shop names, it all seems very familiar. Many shops and businesses remain open until midnight, which means the area is vibrant and busy until late.

Konak Kneginje Ljubice (Princess Ljubica's Konak)

This 19th-century mansion, formerly home to Princess Ljubica, wife of Prince Miloš Obrenović, and her sons, was converted into a museum and is now set up as it might have looked in the past, with various Turkish- and European-influenced furniture and rooms, including a Turkish bathhouse, or *hammam*. There are little nooks and crannies to explore, and a few display cases with costumes, pottery, medals, glasses and goblets. Because there are no written explanations stuck on the walls to remind you that you're in a museum, the whole place has a certain air of authenticity, and if you're lucky enough to visit it when there are hardly any other tourists there, it can be rather fun to walk around imagining life as a royal. ➋ Kneza Sime

◔ *The mighty Orthodox Cathedral*

Markovića 8 🕿 011 263 8264 🕒 10.00–17.00 Tues–Wed, Fri & Sat,
12.00–20.00 Thurs, 10.00–14.00 Sun, closed Mon
🛈 Admission charge

Saborna crkva Sv Arhangela (Orthodox Cathedral or Holy Archangel Michael Church)

Belgrade's cavernous Orthodox Cathedral is as ornate as you
would expect, brimming with gold, red carpets and enormous
chandeliers, plus an elaborate, gold-lined pulpit. It also boasts
its fair share of art, with simple stained-glass windows and
religious scenes covering the main inside wall and the ceiling.
You can stock up on your icons and religious texts from a small
shop at the entrance. 🖻 Kneza Sime Markovića 3 🕿 011 636 684
🕒 07.30–18.00

Seik Mustafino Turbe (Sheik Mustafa's Tomb)

Built over 200 years ago as a mausoleum, the tomb stands as
a rare monument to Turkish rule in the city. 🖻 On the corner of
Braće Jugovića and Višnjićeva, opposite Trg Studentski

Trg Studentski

A quiet city garden with a sprinkling of statues, trees and
benches, Trg Studentski is popular with courting couples,
dog walkers and readers seeking some respite from the
bustle of the town – all things considered, then, this is a great
place for a pit stop. A children's playground in one corner does
not intrude on the peaceful atmosphere, which is perhaps
explained by the park's former incarnation as a cemetery.
The entrance gates are worthy of architectural interest in

their own right, although the statues seem to be used more as unorthodox places for students to get some shut-eye rather than as impressive visual features. **ⓐ** Opposite the Ethnographic Museum

CULTURE

Centar za Grafiku i Vizeulna Istrazivanja (Centre for Graphic Art & Visual Research)

Both a working department and a public gallery, the Centre for Graphic Art & Visual Research is part of the Faculty of Fine Arts, a meeting point for Serbian artists, and has pieces you can view and/or buy as well as a library. Check the website for details of upcoming special exhibitions. **ⓐ** Faculty of Fine Arts, Pariska 16, at junction with Knez Mihailova **ⓣ** 011 328 2800 **ⓦ** www.fluc.org **ⓛ** Gallery: 10.00–19.00 Mon–Fri, 10.00–15.00 Sat

Etno Muzej (Ethnographic Museum)

Spread out over several floors and rooms, the Ethnographic Museum offers a comprehensive overview of 19th- and 20th-century life and culture through the region. The ground floor features mostly traditional rural costumes and photographs, while the upstairs exhibits also reflect the lifestyle of the well-off town set. There's an emphasis on farming and textile production, and various equipment and carpets are on display along with musical instruments, furniture, carts, carriages and small models of buildings. The huge surface area available affords space for mock-up rooms from both rural dwellings and town houses, which reveal the area's competing Turkish and

European influences. Most captions are translated into English. The museum hosts temporary exhibitions, talks, plays, concerts and other promotions. Its website does not post an up-to-date programme, so phone for information. ⓐ Trg Studentski 13 ❶ 011 328 1888 ⓦ www.etnografskimuzej.rs ❷ 10.00–17.00 Tues–Sat, 09.00–14.00 Sun ❶ Admission charge

Galerija Fresaka (Fresco Gallery)

The gallery houses a collection of copies of the country's religious art. Everything – huge murals that practically cover a whole wall, stone carvings, marble tombstones – is in one large exhibition room. There is none of the shoddiness you might normally associate with replicas. ⓐ Cara Uroša 20 ❶ 011 262 1491 ❷ 10.00–17.00 Tues, Wed & Fri, 12.00–20.00 Thur & Sat, 10.00–14.00 Sun

Jevrejski Istorijski Muzej (Jewish Historical Museum)

Featuring a vast collection of photos, documents and artefacts charting Jewish life in the region for over 2,000 years, the museum is tucked away on the first floor of its building. You'll need to ring the bell to get in. Prominent among the many items on show is a sobering display on the Holocaust. ⓐ Kralja Petra 71A ❶ 011 262 2634 ⓦ www.jim-bg.org ❷ 10.00–12.00 Mon–Fri

Muzej nad Odredeni Clan Srpski Pravoslavan Crkva (Museum of the Serbian Orthodox Church)

Right opposite the Orthodox Cathedral, the museum tries to tell the story of Serbian Orthodoxy through icons, woodcarvings, stone engravings, textiles and books, some of which date back

over 500 years. **ⓐ** Kralja Petra 5 **ⓣ** 011 328 2588 **ⓦ** www.spc.rs
ⓛ 08.00–16.00 Mon–Fri, 09.00–12.00 Sat, 11.00–13.00 Sun
ⓘ Admission charge

Muzej Primenjene Umetnosti (Applied Art Museum)

Exhibiting jewellery, icons, prints, photos, textiles, glassware
and ceramics, the chief draw for art lovers may well be the
museum's shop, which sells a range of accessories and pieces
by contemporary Serbian designers. The shop keeps the same
hours as the museum. **ⓐ** 18 Vuka Karadžića **ⓣ** 011 262 6841
ⓦ www.mpu.rs **ⓛ** 11.00–19.00 Tues–Sat **ⓘ** Admission charge

Prirodnjacki Muzej (Natural History Museum Gallery)

Situated in an outhouse of the fortress, this small museum is
well worth a look if you're passing through Kalemegdan Park.
It has lots of information in English on all aspects of Serbian
natural history, and exhibits from leaves and insects to bats and
stuffed birds. The centrepiece of the collection is a huge bearded
vulture with its wings wide open, as if it is about to dive down
on to some poor doomed mouse. There's also a science bit, with
a detailed explanation of the mechanics of flying. A small shop
sells shells, books and jewellery made of stones. **ⓐ** Mali
Kalemegdan 5 **ⓣ** 011 328 4317 **ⓦ** www.nhmbeo.rs **ⓛ** 10.00–17.00
Tues–Sun (winter); 10.00–21.00 daily (summer) **ⓝ** Tram: 2, 11, 13;
Bus: 31 **ⓘ** Admission charge (free on Thur)

Umetnicki paviljon Cvijeta Zuzorić (Cvijeta Zuzorić Art Pavilion)

Members of the Association of Fine Artists of Serbia both exhibit
and sell their work through the art gallery. **ⓐ** Mali Kalemegdan 1

☎ 011 262 1585 ⓦ www.ulus-art.org ⏰ 10.00–20.00 Mon–Fri,
09.00–14.00 Sat

Vojni Muzej (Military Museum)

While most of the places from which tourists hail might be
lacking first-hand experience of conflict, the same cannot be
said of Serbia. Subsequently, as well as the traditional Roman,
Greek and medieval daggers, helmets and armour, the museum
also features more recent exhibits, such as bits of an American
stealth aircraft shot down by the local army in the 1990s.
ⓐ Mali Kalemegdan ☎ 011 334 3441 ⓦ www.muzej.mod.gov.rs
⏰ 10.00–17.00 Tues–Sun ❶ Admission charge

RETAIL THERAPY

Knez Mihailova Glance around Knez Mihailova and you could be
on the main street or boulevard of any sophisticated European
city. Familiar names such as Zara, Mango, Nike, Adidas and
Benetton stand alongside smaller, specialist shops and boutiques.
There is the occasional café, but most of the eateries are down
side streets, perhaps not to intrude too much on the main
business of shopping.

TAKING A BREAK

Caffe Troika £ ❶ Jazzy music and a wooden interior redolent of
a *Columbo* set give this cosy café-bar a welcoming retro feel. The
street is home to a phalanx of bars, so Troika, with its extensive
cocktail list, could also be a starting point for a night on the

tiles. ⓐ Strahinjića Bana 3 🕓 08.00–24.00 Mon–Thur, 08.00–01.00 Fri & Sat, 10.00–24.00 Sun

Via del Gusto £ ❷ Split-level café-restaurant with small, round tables, barstools and a wrought-iron motif. The menu features reasonably priced pastries and cakes as well as light mains, like pizza, pasta and salads. ⓐ Knez Mihailova 48 ❶ 011 328 8200 ⓦ www.viadelgusto.net 🕓 07.30–24.00

Gaston ££ ❸ Cosy and very traditional café/restaurant where the locals pop in for their caffeine fixes and cigarettes. Excellent place around the corner from Knez Mihailova to escape to if it is raining or cold outside. ⓐ Uzun Mirkova 5 ❶ 011 328 5811 ⓦ www.gostionicagaston.com 🕓 09.00–23.00 Mon–Fri, 12.00–23.00 Sat & Sun

AFTER DARK

RESTAURANTS
Freska café restaurant £ ❹ Very highly rated Italian restaurant with a good range of pasta, pizza, salads and meat mains, all for reasonable prices. In warm weather you can eat at an outside table. ⓐ Vuka Karadžića 12, corner with Knez Mihailova ❶ 011 328 4879 🕓 11.00–23.00 Mon–Sat, 12.00–22.00 Sun

'?' ££ ❺ The question mark 'name' of this restaurant, the oldest in the city, is a result of a dispute between it and the Cathedral over the road, which it was once named after. The menu is full of the best Serbian fare Belgrade has to offer and the place is

◔ *Quirky ceramics are among Belgrade's offerings*

a magnet for travellers as well as locals. ⓐ Kralja Petra 6
ⓣ 011 236 5421 ⓛ 08.00–24.00

Peking ££ ⓺ The city's first Chinese restaurant, the highly rated
Peking offers the 100-plus dishes you'd expect. The interior is
decent, but if you prefer to eat elsewhere they also deliver.
ⓐ Vuka Karadzića 2, near Trg Studentski ⓣ 011 218 1931
ⓦ www.peking.co.rs ⓛ 11.00–23.00 Mon–Sat, 13.00–20.00 Sun

Kalemegdanska Terasa £££ ⓻ Takes pride of place right
in the middle of Belgrade's most illustrious landmark and
offers sumptuous views of the Danube from the terrace.
Booking ahead is wise as the restaurant often fills up with
a mass of diners eager to feast on the lavish, traditional
fare on offer. ⓐ Mali Kalemegdan ⓣ 011 328 3011
ⓦ www.kalemegdanskaterasa.com ⓛ 12.00–01.00;
terrace 09.00–04.00

Square Nine £££ ⓼ Exemplary service and an enjoyably grown-
up atmosphere form the backdrop to this top-notch eatery,
where the fine fare includes duck, veal and sea bass, plus lighter
international dishes such as pasta and risotto. There's an
excellent wine list if you want to wash it all down. In the
summer, take your meal on the relaxing terrace. ⓐ Trg
Studentski ⓣ 021 333 3510 ⓦ www.squarenine.rs ⓛ 06.00–10.30,
12.00–16.00, 19.00–23.00

Tribeca £££ ⓽ Attracts a young, trendy crowd, who natter
away quietly to one another while either sipping at their

drinks or tucking into smartly presented international cuisine.
ⓐ Knez Mihailova 50 ⓣ 011 328 5656

BARS & CLUBS

Andergraund Heaving subterranean venue at the foot of
Kalemegdan Park, which treats its punters to all manner of
beats from R&B to house and techno. Unlike most Serbian clubs
there's an entry fee, but it is still light on the pocket. ⓐ Pariska 1A
ⓣ 011 262 5681 ⓛ 10.00–05.00 Wed–Sat

Bar Central Stylish cocktail bar that plays host to the city's
drink-juggling, aspiring Tom Cruises. ⓐ Kralja Petra 59
ⓣ 011 262 6444 ⓦ www.bar.rs (Serbian) ⓛ 09.00–01.00
Mon–Sat, 17.00–01.00 Sun

Havana Just off Knez Mihailova and definitely a place for the
fleet-of-foot, who spin around with relish to the sounds of Latin
America. Salsa and tango dominate the repertoire, but voyeurs
and the simply idle are welcome to prop up the bar while
sampling the club's dizzying range of international drinks.
ⓐ Nikole Spasica 1 ⓣ 011 328 3108 ⓛ 10.00–04.00

CONCERT HALLS
Srpska Akademija Nauka i Umetnosti (Serbian Academy of Sciences & Arts)
The SASA Gallery has a regular programme of free classical
music concerts on Mondays and Thursdays at 18.00 from
October to June. It also hosts art exhibitions. ⓐ Knez Mihailova
35 ⓣ 011 334 2400 ⓦ www.sanu.ac.rs/English

Trg Republike & city centre

Something of a cultural centre, with the National Theatre facing on to it, the pedestrianised Trg Republike is likely to be the starting point for much of your exploration of Belgrade's Old Town. It's constantly busy, peopled by shoppers, strollers and revellers of all ages, and the atmosphere changes by the hour. As well as serving as the site for informal congregation, the square frequently hosts more organised entertainment, which sometimes spills over on to the surrounding streets.

The large junction at Trg Republike serves both as a centre for public transport and as the starting or finishing point for several major Belgrade arteries, including Skadarska, the cobbled hill whose bohemian atmosphere survived NATO's bombs in the 1990s, and Terazije, the main thoroughfare that runs almost north to south. Before it eventually becomes Kralja Milana, Terazije hosts some of the city's landmark hotels, and a few green spaces, one of which is the site of the striking Serbian Federal Parliament building.

Trg Republike and Skadarska are closed to traffic and many of the area's sights are within walking distance of each other. Several trolleybuses also go along Terazije. Driving around the centre is recommended only for the very patient – a confusing network of one-way streets and no-entry junctions can make reaching your destination an exercise in frustration. Far better to jump in a cab or take a wander: some of the anonymous buildings along Belgrade's backstreets are worthy of admiration in their own understated way.

SIGHTS & ATTRACTIONS

Savezni Skupstina zgrada (Federal Parliament building)

One of the most impressive structures in the city – in fact so impressive that it made it on to the country's 5,000-dinar banknote – the Federal Parliament building stands proudly over Pioneers' Park. It was here that demonstrators gathered to

The 19th-century monument to Prince Milhailo dominates Trg Republike

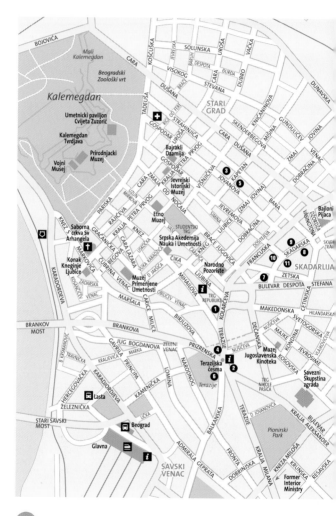

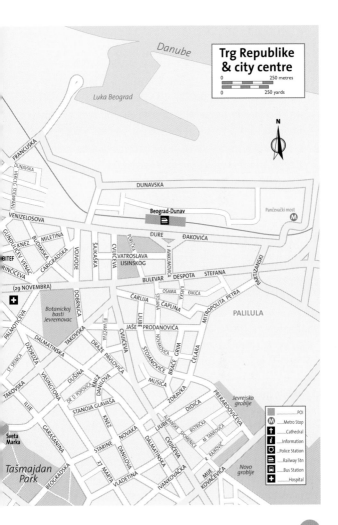

Trg Republike & city centre

0 — 250 metres
0 — 250 yards

N

Danube

Luka Beograd

FRANCUSKA
DUNAVSKA
HERCEG STJEPANU
DUNAVSKA
VENIZELOSOVA
Beograd-Dunav
Pančevački most
ĐURE ĐAKOVIĆA
POŽEGA
KNEZ MILETINA
GUNDULIĆEV VENAC
BUDIMSKA
CARIGRADSKA
VOJVODE
SAJKAŠKA
CVIJIĆEVA
VATROSLAVA LISINSKOG
AVAKUMOVIĆA
BITEF
PRINCIČEVA
BULEVAR DESPOTA STEFANA
PARTIZANSKI
(29 NOVEMBRA)
DOBRNICA
OSAMA
STOJANA
TESLA
ĐIKIĆA
ČARLIJA
ČAPLINA
MITROPOLITA PETRA
PALILULA
Botanickoj basti Jevremovac
PALMOTIĆEVA
ĐURJAČEVA
JAŠE PRODANOVIĆA
LJUBE
NOVAKOVIĆA
ČELARA
DALMATINSKA
TAKOVSKA
DRAŽE PAVLOVIĆA
CVIJIĆEVA
STOJANOVIĆE
BRAĆE GRIM
DŽORDŽA
ST. SRKIĆA
VAŠINGTONA
DUŠINA
DR. D. POPOVIĆA
KNEZ DANILOVA
MUSIĆA
TAKOVSKA
ILIJE
STANOJA GLAVAŠA
ZDRAVKA DIDIĆA
PRERADOVIĆEVA
Jevrejsko groblje
Sveta Marka
GARAŠANINA
KNEZ
NOVAKA
STARINE
DANILOVA
DALMATINSKA
CVIJIĆEVA
ALBANSKE SPOMENICE
BIRČICKA
M. TANKOSIĆA
R. RAJKOVIĆ
Novo groblje
Tašmajdan Park
BEOGRADSKA
27 MARTA
VLADETINA
IVANKOVAČKA
MIJE KOVAČEVIĆA

██ ......POI
Ⓜ ......Metro Stop
✝ ......Cathedral
ℹ ......Information
🛡 ......Police Station
🚉 ......Railway Stn
🚌 ......Bus Station
✚ ......Hospital

79

PARLIAMENT

On 5 October 2000, the Yugoslav Parliament building (now called the Federal Parliament building) was the scene of a demonstration that was the last nail in Milošević's political coffin. When he managed to secure one more year in power after having his defeat in the previous month's presidential election overturned, 900,000 people took to the streets of Belgrade to protest, with many ending up at Parliament. They bulldozed their way into the building and smashed up – or removed – the furniture. At first police fired tear gas at the crowd, but they later withdrew and some officers even joined the protestors. The ground was left littered with the fraudulent voting slips filled in by Milošević's minions. The next day the hated despot stood down and opposition candidate Vojislav Kostunica took office.

protest against the Milošević regime in 2000. ⓐ Trg Nikole Pašića ⓒ 1st Sat each month ⓝ Bus: 26, 37 ⓘ Advance booking required; contact tourist information office

Skadarlija quarter

The first settlers in Skadarlija, the narrow, hilly streets centred on Skadarska, were Roma, or gypsies, and today the district still retains something of their unorthodox style. Supplanting the Roma were craftsmen, and the area soon became popular among the city's bohemian set, as artists and writers gathered to shoot the breeze in Skadarska's old hostelries, some of which are still operating. Today it is colonised by entrepreneurs who, realising that bohemia sells, have re-created it as a tourist area, lined with traditional and modern restaurants, many of which employ gypsy bands to perform live most nights. Some even station their waiters in the street, Turkish style, to persuade you to go in. You can also pick up craft items from the stalls that sometimes set up on the street. Skadarlija might represent Belgrade's first foray into catering for its foreign visitors, but it is still a world away from the cynical tourist traps you find in many developed cities. If you're going out for dinner, forget the heels – cobbled Skadarska is difficult enough to navigate in trainers.

Terazije

The official centre of the city – even if for practical purposes this mantle usually goes to Trg Republike or Kalemegdan – Terazije, both a square and a street in its own right, is one of the city's main shopping areas. It also boasts some of its more notable

○ *The cobbled streets of Skadarlija*

buildings, from the stylish, Art Nouveau Hotel Moskva, now a hundred years old, to the largest McDonald's in the Balkans, a more dubious claimant for honour. The other landmark of note is the Terazijska česma (Terazije Fountain), which is back in its original location after a 65-year sojourn in Topčider Park. The fountain has a spiritual significance for Belgrade's Orthodox Christians, as worshippers stop to pray here during their Ascension Day procession. ⓝ Trolleybus: 19, 21, 22, 29; bus: 31

Trg Republike

The centre of the centre, Trg Republike acts as a microcosm of Belgrade life: whether it's teenagers on their way to a big night out, revellers dancing or nodding along to one of the many concerts staged in front of the National Museum, crocodile lines of children streaming across the square on a school trip or adults taking a few minutes' time out on the benches for a chat or a read, something is always happening here.

CULTURE

Muzej Jugoslavenska Kinoteka (Museum of Yugoslav Cinema)

The museum houses the Yugoslav Film Archives and screens titles from its vast collection. There is something on almost every day, sometimes two or three shows, and the sheer variety will certainly impress film buffs: you could be watching a 90-year-old silent film, a classic from the 1940s or the latest Serbian offering – make sure you check beforehand what language it will be in. The entrance hall hosts exhibitions that have links

TERROR TACTICS

You can't miss the former Interior Ministry building on the corner of Kneza Miloša and Nemarijina. It's not your conventional tourist attraction by any means, but this – along with other state-owned buildings from the Milošević era in the city – is one of the most striking structures you'll ever see, precisely because it is falling to bits. Strafed by NATO in 1999, the building looks as if a giant hand has reached in and torn out its innards. Wounds gape where windows used to be and cables hang down 'inside' like jungle creepers. It'll send a shiver down your spine, which one suspects is why the ruined structure is allowed to remain. Another European lesson – and the most recent at that – on the terror that war unleashes.

with the films being screened. Though the website is in Serbian, film titles are translated into English. ⓐ Kosovska 11 ☏ 011 324 8250 ⓦ www.kinoteka.org.rs ⏱ Varies depending on film schedule; see website ⓥ Trolleybus: 19, 21, 22, 29; bus: 31 ❶ Admission charge

RETAIL THERAPY

Bajlonijeva Pijaca An open-air market at the end of Skadarska, Bajlonijeva Pijaca offers an entirely different shopping experience from the swish boutiques and designer names of Knez Mihailova or the city's undercover malls. Aside from food, you can also pick up odd bric-a-brac, and the adjoining Roma flea market offers sundry items laid out on blankets at low prices. If you want your shopping cheap and colourful, this is the place. ⓐ Off Džordža Vasingtona ① 011 322 3472 ① 07.00–16.00 ⓝ Tram: 2, 5, 10; bus: 24, 26

TAKING A BREAK

Aurelio Café £ ❶ This vibrant eatery bang in the centre of the action busily rustles up sandwiches, salads, cakes and coffees, which can be enjoyed on the large terrace in the square. There's also a takeaway menu. ⓐ Trg Republike 3 ① 063 117 7294 ⓦ www.aurelio.co.rs ① 07.00–24.00

Biblioteka ££ ❷ The name means 'library', but despite the books stacked up on shelves all over the place, there's little that's dusty and sombre about this restaurant. That said, the mood – like in many places in Belgrade – is laid-back and reflective, so perhaps there is a studious air about the smart young crowd that gathers here. ⓐ Terazije 27 ① 011 303 7450 ① 07.30–24.00 Mon–Thur, 07.30–01.00 Fri & Sat, 09.00–24.00 Sun ⓝ Trolleybus: 19, 21, 22, 29; bus: 31

Kandahar ££ ❸ As the name implies, there is a strong Eastern feel to this café on the 'Silicon Valley' strip, where all the beautiful young things hang out at the weekend. Boasts a wide range of teas and genuine Turkish coffee on its drinks menu, as well as ample cushions to give you a real sense of the Orient. ⓐ Strahinjica Bana 48 ① 011 291 0311 ① 09.00–02.00

Kasina ££ ❹ Spacious hangout beneath the hotel of the same name. Brews its own beer and packs in regulars and passers-by. Earthier than next-door neighbour Biblioteka, but competes on level terms when summer arrives and Belgrade goes alfresco. ⓐ Terazije 25 ⓣ 011 325 5574 ⓦ http://kasina-belgrade.hotel-rn.com ⓛ 07.00–23.00 ⓝ Trolleybus: 19, 21, 22, 29; bus: 31

Bistro Pastis £££ ❺ Situated in the notorious 'Silicon Valley' district of cafés, bars and restaurants, this is where Serbia's A-list celebrities gravitate towards when they are not making themselves look gorgeous. The place to look and be looked at, whatever the time of the day. ⓐ Strahinjica Bana 52B ⓣ 011 328 8188 ⓛ 09.00–02.00 Mon–Sat, 10.00–02.00 Sun

Hotel Moskva £££ ❻ A grand way to while away one's time when in Belgrade is to come here and take the weight off. The huge café is populated by plenty of laid-back locals as well as hotel guests, who either chat amiably or take in the swathe of humanity rushing about outside. ⓐ Balkanska 1 ⓣ 011 268 6255 ⓦ www.hotelmoskva.rs ⓛ 06.30–23.00 ⓝ Trolleybus: 19, 21, 22, 29; bus: 31

AFTER DARK

RESTAURANTS
Campo de Fiori ££ ❼ Serves up Italian staples in a modern environment. One of several good Italian restaurants in the area. ⓐ Skadarska 11 ⓣ 011 324 2940 ⓦ www.campodefiori.rs ⓛ 11.00–23.00

Dva Jelena ££ ❽ Attention all carnivores: this place has meaty specialities such as venison. But it also offers separate tourist and vegetarian menus. There are murals on the walls and entertainment most nights. ⓐ Skadarska 32 ❶ 011 323 4885 ❶ 11.00–01.00

Guli ££ ❾ Watch your pizza being cooked, or try one of the enjoyable pasta dishes at this modern and intimate Italian, which is simply but stylishly decorated. ⓐ Skadarska 13 ❶ 011 323 7204 ⓦ www.guli.rs ❶ 12.00–23.30

Sesir Moj ££ ❿ Lots of meaty Serbian treats for ravenous carnivores in here, with a mass of striking oil paintings on the walls to keep you curious as you tuck into the wholesome grub. Very attentive and polite service to boot. ⓐ Skadarska 21 ❶ 011 322 8750 ⓔ sesir.moj@skadarlija.rs ❶ 11.00–01.00 Mon–Sat

Zlatan Bokal ££ ⓫ One of the grandes dames of Skadarska eateries, this traditional place has an atmosphere that recalls yesteryear – if not yester-century – and hosts regular entertainment. ⓐ Skadarska 26 ❶ 011 323 4834 ❶ 11.00–01.00

BARS & CLUBS

Apartman You might think a highly ambitious and raucous house party is going on in here if you happen to be wandering by on the nearby Branko Bridge, as the club is located in a converted apartment which you reach by ascending a steep staircase. This gay-friendly venue holds regular theme nights. ⓐ Karadjordjeva 43 ❶ 065 846 8467 ❶ 23.00–05.00 Fri & Sat ⓝ Tram: 2

Noir Lounge and Night Club Chill-out lounge by day, achingly trendy house club by night, monochrome Noir also boasts an unbeatable spot overlooking Trg Republike. ⓐ Trg Republike 5 ⓣ 060 050 4039 ⓦ www.noir.rs

Red Bar A modern bar where the clientele come to sip drinks rather than sit among the diners amassed in the numerous restaurants close by. You might grab a bar stool if you are lucky and enjoy a chat with the barman. ⓐ Skadarska 17 ⓛ 11.00–02.00

The Three Carrots Irish Pub Belgrade's first ever Irish pub lives up to its theme well in terms of décor and availability of Guinness (though at quite a high price). But it is as an establishment promoting conviviality that it scores highest. ⓐ Kneza Miloša 16 ⓣ 011 268 3748 ⓦ www.threecarrots.co.rs ⓛ 10.00–02.00 ⓝ Trolleybus: 19, 21, 22, 29; bus: 31

THEATRE
BITEF Teatar (BITEF Theatre) Housed in a former church, the BITEF Theatre hosts the Belgrade International Theatre Festival, as well as numerous other shows throughout the year, including the odd one in English. Details are on its website. ⓐ Skver Mire Trailovic ⓣ 011 324 3108 ⓦ www.bitef.rs ⓛ Box office: 15.00–20.00

Narodno Pozoriste (National Theatre) Plays in English at Belgrade's oldest and biggest theatre are few and far between, but the venue also hosts opera and ballet. Consult the theatre website for events. ⓐ Francuska 3, overlooking Trg Republike ⓣ 011 328 1333 ⓦ www.narodnopozoriste.co.rs

South Belgrade

While the south of the city is not as crowded with places of interest as the centre, it has some of the most famous ones. Across the road from Parliament (Savezni Skupstina zgrada) is Tašmajdan Park, one of several green spaces outside the bustle of the Old Town. The park is home to St Mark's Church, but the most impressive religious building in the area is St Sava's Church, which dominates Belgrade's skyline and provides a useful orientation point. Heading further south you come to a cluster of attractions that encapsulate very different aspects of Belgrade life. The street of embassies – complete with armed guards – showcases the city's elite and the strikingly diverse architecture of their houses. Close by are the stadiums that are home to football giant Red Star and its lesser-known rival Partizan, which in turn are just a few minutes away – although a different world in terms of atmosphere – from Tito's tomb. This peaceful mausoleum forms part of the same complex – the House of Flowers Tito Memorial Complex – as a museum that has on display some of the many weird and wonderful gifts bestowed upon the Yugoslav president by foreign dignitaries.

The sights of southern Belgrade are fairly disparate, so a car – or taxi – might come in useful, although buses do also go as far as the football stadiums and the Tito Memorial Complex.

SIGHTS & ATTRACTIONS

Ada Ciganlija

When the sun is out, Belgraders flock to the river island of Ada Ciganlija. The place is essentially devoted to leisure.

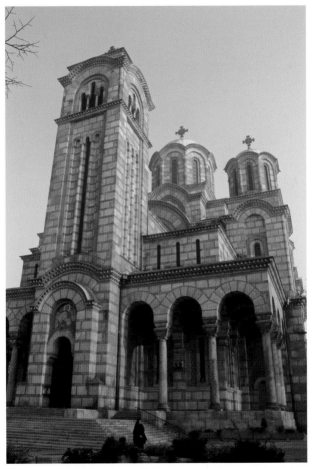

 The Byzantine exterior of St Mark's

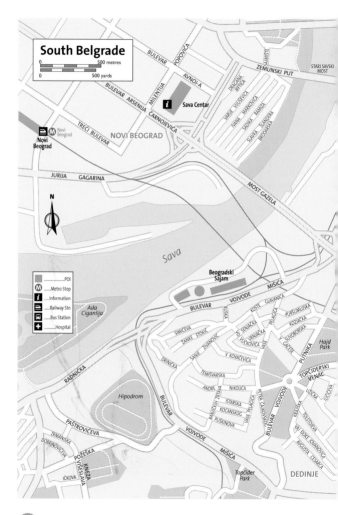

South Belgrade

0 — 500 metres
0 — 500 yards

BULEVAR
POPOVCA
ZEMUNSKI PUT
STARI SAVSKI MOST
AVNOJA
MILENTIJA
Sava Centar
BULEVAR ARSENIJA ČARNOJEVIĆA
DRAGANA JEFTICA
VARJE VUISEVICA
ILIANA MARKOVCA
SADIKA RAMIJA
SLAVKA SLANGERA
BRODARSKA
TRECI BULEVAR
NOVI BEOGRAD
Novi Beograd
Novi Beograd

JURIJA GAGARINA
MOST GAZELA

N

Sava

Beogradski Sajam
MISICA
BULEVAR VOJVODE
RUSKA KOSTE GLAVANICA
PELAGICA PURSUMLIJSKA
KOZJACKA
Ada Ciganlija
SIMICEVA
ZANKE STOKIC
SENJACKA
VOJ VUCKOVICA
VRNJACKA
JASE
SVJOBORSKA
SVJACKE
DRINICKA
ZANKE ŽIVANOVIC
V. KOVACEVICA
PUTNIKA
Hajd Park
V. KOVACEVICA
TEMISVARSKA
ANDRE NIKOLICA
TOPCIDERSKI VENAC
RADNICKA
PERA CANOVSKO
BARUICH ZENIA
ISTARSKA
BULEVAR VOJVODE
UZICKA
JASE PELAGICA
KOCANSKOG
KNEZA
TOSTERA
Hipodrom
BULEVAR
PUSKINOVA
VAT DOKE JOVANOVICA
VJCEVA
PASTROVICEVA
VOJVODE MISICA
AUGUSTA CESARCA
ZERMANJSKA
DOBRINOVICEVA
Topcider Park
DEDINJE
POŽEŠKA
VISEGRADA
ICKOVA

Legend

- POI
- Metro Stop
- Information
- Railway Stn
- Bus Station
- Hospital

Visitors can choose to enjoy the relaxing pastimes of swimming, sunbathing (there's a nude beach for those intent on avoiding a tan line) and having a break in a café, or go for the more adrenalin-fuelled end of the spectrum by taking part in extreme pursuits like bungee jumping.

On top of that you can do almost any sport you can think of, as well as rent bicycles, play mini-golf, go shopping – the island is like a holiday resort within a city. ⓐ In the Sava River ⓝ Bus: 55, 56, 92; ferry from Novi Beograd ⓘ Be warned: as it is so popular, it can get crowded

Botanickoj basti Jevremovac (Jevremovac Botanical Gardens)

Part of Belgrade University's Faculty of Biology, the gardens are home to about 300 kinds of trees, bushes and plants and are a pleasant place for a walk even if you can't tell your *lactuca sativa* from your *lactuca muralis*. ⓐ Takovska 43 ⓣ 011 324 4847 ⓛ 09.00–19.00, 1 May–1 Nov ⓝ Bus: 16, 27E, 32E, 35, 43 ⓘ Admission charge

Kuća Cveća (Tito Memorial Complex or House of Flowers)

A gem of an attraction that for some reason – perhaps because it's some way from the centre, or perhaps because the idea of going to visit a dead dictator is not everyone's cup of tea – sees relatively few visitors. The complex consists of three buildings, the largest of which was once a museum of artefacts on the life of Josip Broz Tito, who was in office, first as prime minister and then as president, for some 35 years. Now, though, as well as two presidential motorcars in the foyer, it hosts occasional exhibitions and special events.

Up the hill, and with a wonderful view over the city, lies Tito's tomb, a peaceful and dignified resting place for the Yugoslav leader. A red carpet and velvet curtains create an almost regal atmosphere, and the tomb itself is light marble, surrounded by plants, which stop the place from feeling depressing. Aside from the central hall, the building contains several other rooms, including one housing a collection of batons that were used in ceremonies on the president's birthdays. The Chinese parlour contains ornate antique furniture, embroidered carpet and a chandelier.

But the best bit of the whole complex is the museum near the tomb, which displays some of the diplomatic donations that Tito was given over the course of his 35 years in power. It's an astonishing collection: there are costumes, dolls, musical instruments, saddles and all manner of weapons – everything the modern president might want. A highlight of the collection is a marvellous Bolivian witch-doctor costume, complete with colourful mask. ⓐ Botičeva 6 ⓣ 011 367 1296 ⓦ www.mij.rs ⓛ 09.00–16.00 Tues–Sun ⓜ Trolleybus: 40, 41; bus: 94 ⓘ Admission charge

Stadion Crvena Zvezda & Stadion Partizana (Red Star & Partizan Belgrade stadiums)

Football rivalries don't get much more hostile than Red Star and Partizan Belgrade; their derby game is known as *veciti derbi*, the 'eternal derby'. In the past the rivalry has erupted into violence, but today things are usually more composed. Even so, football matches in Serbia are seldom genteel affairs. If you're visiting Belgrade during the football season and your trip coincides with a fixture, it can be quite an experience. Matches rarely sell out –

● *Pick up footballing souvenirs at the Red Star shop*

although of course a big game could be an exception – and you should be able to pick up a ticket at the ground. If you're not a fan of football, the two clubs also field teams in other disciplines such as hockey, water polo, handball, basketball and even rowing, so there is plenty of choice for spectators. Both Red Star and Partizan also have modern and well-stocked shops where you can find various memorabilia. Red Star even has a museum, where past trophies, newspaper cuttings and photos are on show.

FC Crvena Zvezda (Red Star) ⓐ Ljutice Bogdana 1A
ⓦ www.crvenazvezdafk.com ⓝ Trolleybus: 40, 41
Club museum ⓣ 011 367 2060 ⓛ 09.00–16.00 Mon–Fri,
09.00–14.00 Sat
Club shop ⓛ 09.00–19.00 Mon–Fri, 09.00–15.00 Sat
Partizan ⓐ Humska 1, near Tito Memorial complex ⓣ 011 369 3336
ⓦ www.partizan.rs ⓛ Club shop: 09.00–17.00 Mon–Fri,
10.00–15.00 Sat

Street of embassies

The street of embassies gives you an idea of a different Belgrade. An eclectic row of expensive diplomatic houses, with the flags of various nations hanging from each, it's an interesting drive or walk both for those interested in architecture and for anybody who enjoys seeing how the other half lives. With armed guards outside, though, it's a brave tourist who stops and takes a picture. Unfortunately, you can't go into the buildings – unless you're going to report a lost passport perhaps – so you won't have an excuse to spend long on the street, but it's on the way from the centre of the city to the Tito Memorial Complex and the two football stadiums, and it's worth making a brief detour here during the daytime. ⓐ Birčaninova ⓝ Trolleybus: 40, 41; bus: 23, 37, 44, 53, 56, 58, 92

Sveta Marka (St Mark's Church)

Built to replace a previous church on the site, red and yellow St Mark's is a copy of the hallowed Kosovan Gracanica Monastery. Byzantine in style on the outside, the interior contains a selection of 18th- and 19th-century icons. ⓐ Bulevar Kralja Aleksander 17 ⓣ 011 323 1940 ⓦ www.crkvasvetogmarka.rs ⓛ 07.00–19.00 ⓝ Tram: 3, 6, 7L

Sveti Sava (St Sava's Church)

Huge, imposing and awe-inspiring – and St Sava's isn't even finished. Despite preparations beginning back at the tail end of the 19th century, the turmoil and upheaval that Belgrade has undergone repeatedly interrupted building work. Only now is the end in sight, with exterior work completed. The interior of the huge church is still undergoing construction, but you can still enter to visit, worship, or light a candle. Even just viewed from the exterior, the sheer size of the thing is enough to impress even the most ardent atheist. Once finished, it is expected to be the third-largest Orthodox building in the world – unless another massive church gets built in the meantime, which is not inconceivable given the snail's pace at which work has progressed.

The church is set in beautifully sculptured gardens with several statues, and it's a charming place to sit and relax, independent of the magnificent view you enjoy. Next to St Sava's is a small Orthodox church that sees far more worshippers than tourists. Of course it pales in comparison to the monolith by which it stands, but it's a pretty, pleasant place of worship and – in the absence of a completed interior at St Sava's – the simple murals, marble floor and crown-line chandelier are a decent substitute. Watching the churchgoers also gives you a good idea of the demonstrative requirements of Orthodoxy, such as kissing

⬤ *The dramatic contours of St Sava's*

the various icons. 🅐 Krušedolska 2 ❶ 011 243 2585
🕓 08.00–15.00 Ⓝ Bus: 47, 48

Tašmajdan Park

Tašmajdan Park is another of those agreeable green spaces that
Belgraders enjoy killing time in. Today it is famous for nothing
more ominous than the Honey Fair that takes place there each
October, but, as is true of much of modern Belgrade, its history
is less sweet. The Romans buried their dead here, although the
graves were subsequently moved. The vacated chambers were
later used to store military supplies and as a place in which to
tend to wounded soldiers. If you're interested in seeing the
underground network, one of the city's tourist information offices
should be able to arrange it if given advance notice. Named after
the quarry that previously occupied the site under the Ottomans,
the park was bombed by the Nazis in 1941 and again by NATO in
1999. Tašmajdan now hosts a monument to all the children who
died in the NATO campaign. Shaped like a heart, it reads, 'We were
just children', in both Serbian and English.

As well as St Mark's Church (see page 95), the park is also
home to a sports centre with a couple of swimming pools.
There are a couple of cafés in the park if you want to linger
over refreshments. 🅐 Bulevar Kralja Aleksander Ⓝ Tram: 7L, 12

Topčider Park

Like many of the city's parks, Topčider – the oldest one – also
has a military history. Today, the huge green area is far more
peaceful, hosting the Historical Museum of Serbia (🕓 09.00–
17.00 Tues–Sun) in the mansion that Prince Miloš Obrenović

built for himself, as well as a few monuments, including an obelisk. Despite its peaceful aspect, however, rumours persist following the discovery of a network of tunnels underneath the park, built at the command of Tito who feared nuclear attack by the Russians. As well as being used as a war bunker by Milošević during the NATO campaign, the tunnels are said to have provided sanctuary to other renegades from the law.
ⓐ South of Bulevar Vojvode Mišića Ⓝ Trolleybus: 40, 41; bus: 49

CULTURE

Muzej nad Koncentracijski logor Banjica (Banjica Concentration Camp Museum)

Sobering display of photos and personal effects chronicling the history of the Nazi death camp that formerly occupied the site. ⓐ Pavla Jurišića Šturma 33 ⓣ 011 263 0825 ⓦ www.mgb.org.rs ⓛ 10.00–16.00 Tues & Sat Ⓝ Trolleybus: 40, 41 ❶ Admission charge

Studentski Kulturni Centar (Students' Cultural Centre)

The institute organises a growing programme of theatre, music, art and literature events. ⓐ Kralja Milana 48 ⓣ 011 360 2009 ⓦ www.skc.org.rs (Serbian) Ⓝ Trolleybus: 19, 21, 22, 29; bus: 31

RETAIL THERAPY

Beogradski Sajam (Belgrade Fair)
The events, fairs and shows staged here run the gamut from the usual suspects such as fashion, cars, furniture, technology and books, to the less

ordinary – an erotic fair premiered in 2005. From time to time you can also catch a concert. Several halls have been permanently given over to shopping. Known as the bazaar, it sells clothes, food, cosmetics and other day-to-day items and is open seven days a week. ⓐ Bulevar Vojvode Mišića 14, by the Sava ⓣ 011 265 5555 ⓦ www.sajam.co.rs ⓛ 10.00–20.00 outside fair time; 10.00–19.00 during fairs ⓝ Bus: 23, 52, 53, 56

Kalenić Pijaca As well as fruit and veg, Kalenic Pijaca sells antiques, old books, Communist-era memorabilia and a wealth of other bric-a-brac and is a good place to pick up some quirky presents and souvenirs. If you can, go on Friday or Saturday morning when it's at its most bustling. ⓐ Njegoševa (not far from St Sava's Church) ⓛ 07.00 or 08.00–15.00 or 16.00 ⓝ Bus: 25, 26

TAKING A BREAK

Ilije Garašanina, which runs alongside Tašmajdan Park to the northeast, is home to a little café district with about four outlets serving drinks and ice cream in a line. Two of the best are listed below:

Caffe Pool £ ❶ Modern, minimalist and classy, Pool is one of the better choices in this area with friendly and helpful staff. ⓐ 33 Ilije Garašanina ⓛ 08.00–24.00 ⓝ Tram: 7

Loligo £ ❷ With green décor, an outside terrace and obliging staff, Loligo is a cosy spot in which to avail yourself of refreshments. ⓐ 29 Ilije Garašanina ⓛ 08.00–23.00 ⓝ Tram: 7

AFTER DARK

RESTAURANTS

Orac £ ❸ So popular that they have a marquee extension to house any overflow customers. The day menu – though only in Serbian – consists of some excellent local dishes at very reasonable prices, and the other meals (which are described in English) can be highly recommended as well. ⓐ Makenzijeva 81 ❶ 011 243 0885 🕒 09.00–24.00 Ⓝ Trolleybus: 40, 19; bus: 65, 77

Byblos ££ ❹ Byblos is a rare thing: a small Lebanese restaurant in Serbia. It offers the usual dishes such as hummus, montabel, kebabs and so on. The service is warm and attention is paid to vegetarians. You may also catch the belly dancer. ⓐ Kneginje Zorke 30, near Trg Slavija ❶ 011 244 1938 🕒 12.00–24.00 Ⓝ Trolleybus: 19, 21, 22; bus: 26

Kalenić ££ ❺ Close to the market of the same name, this large restaurant has built its reputation by offering simple Serbian fare. In warm weather, you can eat outside. ⓐ Mileševska 2 ❶ 011 245 0666 🕒 08.00–24.00

BARS & CLUBS

Bukowski Bar It sounds more like something from Belgrade, Montana, rather than Belgrade, Serbia, but the tiny Bukowski café bar still survives and prospers. ⓐ Kičevska 6, near the Vuk monument in Student's Park ❶ 011 243 6796 Ⓝ Tram: 7; bus: 25, 26

🔾 *The spire of St Mary's, Novi Sad*

OUT OF TOWN
trips

Novi Beograd & Zemun

Technically Novi Beograd (New Belgrade) is part of the town. But sitting across the river with its austere, modern buildings it feels wholly distinct from the centre and very much has its own identity. While the area's monotonous 1960s blocks have been slated in songs and films, parts of the area on the other side of the Sava have real character, such as Zemun, a pretty little place that was once under Austrian control.

Previously an entirely separate town, Zemun has been sucked into the city limits and is now officially a municipality of Belgrade. But it retains a distinctive identity and wandering around its pretty streets, with their slow, almost sleepy way of life, you'll feel miles away from a capital city. It's older than Belgrade and has managed to avoid some of the capital's misfortunes: Zemun was in fact quite prosperous, which is clear from the smart and brightly coloured 18th- and 19th-century buildings that remain in excellent condition.

GETTING THERE

Several bridges connect Novi Beograd with the city centre (see map pages 50–51). Although it lies just the other side of the Sava, getting there is not always straightforward – if you're driving, the bridge systems and various turn-offs can be confusing. There are no trolleybuses that side of the river, but a handful of trams crosses over, or you can take a train – or one of more than 20 buses – over either Gazela, Stari Savski or Brankov most (bridge).

◐ *St Nicholas Church and the rooftops of Zemun*

Belgrade region

0   10 km
0   6 miles

Kula

Budapest

Vrbas

Srbobran

Odžaci

A22

7

VOJVODINA

Temerin

Vukovar

Kać

Danube

Petrovaradinsk
Tvrdava

Vinkovki

Bačka
Palanka

Futog

NOVI SAD

CROATIA

Fruška Gora

Sremska
Kamenica

Sremsk
Karlovc

Zagreb

Šid

Nacionalni Park
Fruška Gora

Crveni Čot
539

Iriski
Venac

21

A1

Ruma

E7C

Laćarak

Sremska
Mitrovica

Sava

Bijelina

Drina

Šabac

Sava

BOSNIA
HERZEGOVINA

19

○ ....City
○ ....Large Town
○ ....Small Town
▪ ....POI
........Motorway
....Main Road
....Minor Road
✈ ....Airport
............Railway
....International
Border

Loznica

Koceljevo

Zvornik

104

SIGHTS & ATTRACTIONS

Zemun

One thing that Zemun does not lack is churches, most of which were built in the 18th century. Some of them have fared better than others, but the majority are open to the public and worth popping into. There are so many in such a small space that you're bound to pass some even if you walk aimlessly, but if you're particularly keen not to miss any, the **tourist information office** (ⓐ Zmaj Jovina 14 ⓣ 011 219 2094 ⓛ 09.00–12.00, 16.00–18.00 ⓝ Bus: 15–17, 73, 83, 84, 703–6) has a map that pinpoints them all.

The other main points of interest are all within walking distance of each other, so the best way to see them is just to have a slow wander around and take in the sights, such as Sundial House, on the corner of Dubrovacka and Glavna, and Sibinjanin Janko Tower on Gardos Hill, Grobljanska. The Millennium Tower, as it's also known, can be seen from the other side of the river. For maps and suggestions, try the tourist office.

Flea market

From fruit, veg, meat and fish to clothes, mobile phones and all manner of household and garden items and tools, Zemun's flea market covers a huge area and, with its narrow lanes and haggard traders, it's about as far from a tourist trap as you can get. ⓐ Off Gospodska, Zemun ⓛ 07.00–19.00

TURBO-FOLK

Turbo-folk is something of a contradiction in terms: a blend of turbo – or high-energy, modern dance beats – and old-fashioned Serbian folk music. Although the name has been about since the late 1980s, it was in 1993 that it resurfaced with a vengeance. Against the backdrop of the Balkan wars and their resulting hardships, Serbs were looking for both national reaffirmation and escapism from their country's plight – and they found them in music. The BBC summed it up, reporting that 'In 1990s Serbia, there were two things on the radio: one of them was war and the other was turbo-folk.' With Middle Eastern, Roma, Turkish and Greek influences plus dashes of rock and roll, dance, soul, house and garage, the music was raunchy and provocative. Massive in Serbia, turbo-folk quickly spread round the rest of the Balkans.

It was soon attracting criticism from various quarters, derided by many as lowbrow, tacky, pornographised and glorifying violence and crime. Left-wingers denounced it as xenophobic, a sop to detract the masses from the war; those on the right bemoaned its 'un-European' Turkish and Islamic influences. But the phenomenon has defied its detractors, retaining its popularity long after the end of the hostilities that spawned it. Tens of thousands of fans attend the concerts, and CDs and DVDs of the music are among the country's bestsellers. Turbo-folk can also be heard – usually rather loudly – in the floating clubs, or *splavovi*, of Novi Beograd (see pages 108 & 112).

Floating clubs & restaurants

Novi Beograd's floating nightlife is legendary. First you eat, in one of the many excellent seafood restaurants either on – or right by – the river. After your meal, it's time to hit the *splavovi*, or floating dance clubs. Eastern Europe and the Balkans might not be top of the list when you think of the hippest party destinations, but the Belgrade scene pulls in big-name DJs, and young Belgraders take their revelry very seriously. If you really want to go local, you must fit in some turbo-folk (see page 107). Some venues are included here in the After Dark listings (see pages 111–112) – otherwise, just take a walk along the river and see which of the venues takes your fancy.

⬤ *Altarpiece at the Zemun Museum*

Hala Sportova (Sports Hall)

Not, as the name suggests, exclusively dedicated to sport, the arena also stages concerts. Kings of Leon and Elbow have played the venue and other acts to grace the stage include Blondie, Paul Anka and local band Hladno Pivo (Cold Beer). ⓐ Pariske Komune 20, Novi Beograd ⓣ 011 260 1658

River cruises

Departing from near the now-defunct Hotel Jugoslavia (see map pages 50–51), Zemun or a couple of other embarkation points, there is a choice of itineraries that take in Veliko Ratno island, Kalemegdan, the Orthodox Cathedral and Ada Ciganlija among other highlights. Lunch and dinner cruises are operated, and you can be on the water from anywhere between one hour and ten. From time to time you can also take a party cruise at night. Book your place with the Tourist Organisation of Belgrade; the various options are listed on its website.

CULTURE

Muzej Savremene Umetnosti (Museum of Contemporary Art)

Housing a vast array of 20th-century Serbian paintings and sculpture, the museum's collection features works of Surrealism, Expressionism and Critical Realism. One of the interesting things to do in this absorbing gallery is trace Belgrade's recent history through the pictures, from the resistance during World War II to a laudatory portrait of Tito. There are sub-collections of pre- and post-1945 sculptures, prints, drawings and new art media, and the museum hosts films, openings and other events.

ⓐ Ušće 10, Blok 15, Novi Beograd ⓣ 011 311 5713 ⓦ www.msub.
org.rs ⓛ 10.00–17.00 Wed–Mon (winter); 10.00–18.00
Wed–Mon (summer) ⓝ Bus: 60 ⓘ Admission charge

Muzej Zemun (Zemun Museum)
This is the place to go if you want to learn more about how
Zemun originated and developed, starting way back in
prehistoric times. The museum is currently closed for long-term
renovation. ⓐ Glavna 9, Zemun ⓣ 011 316 5234 ⓛ 09.00–16.00
Tues–Fri, 08.00–15.00 Sat & Sun

TAKING A BREAK

Cream Caffe £ A charming and civilised option, with pale yellow
walls creating the genteel atmosphere of a tea room. A great
range of coffees, cakes, biscuits and drinks, including some
domestic wines, served by cheerful and professional staff.
ⓐ Gospodska 26, Zemun ⓣ 064 149 6134/011 316 7054
ⓛ 08.00–24.00 Mon–Sat, 10.00–24.00 Sun

Dalton £ White leather seats and a big plasma television
characterise the ethos of this café-bar. But those in search of
serenity can sit on the terrace overlooking some calming fountains.
ⓐ Glavna 21, Zemun ⓛ 08.00–24.00 Mon–Sat, 09.00–24.00 Sun

Poslastičarnica Sara £ A large and shady terrace is the big draw
on sunny days for this place, where a plethora of cakes, ice cream
and coffee is served up by good-natured staff. ⓐ Gospodska
ⓛ 08.00–23.00

110

AFTER DARK

RESTAURANTS

Novi Beograd and Zemun are home to some of the city's top fish restaurants. Take a drive or walk along Kej Oslobodjenja and you will be spoilt for choice.

La Gondola ££ A list of Italian eats as long as your arm is prepared under the auspices of a genuine Venetian chef. Like its neighbours, the terrace affords splendid river views. ⓐ Kej Oslobodjenja 49, Zemun ⓣ 011 219 9462 ⓛ 11.00–24.00

Kod Kapetana ££ One of the many fine fish restaurants overlooking the Danube. As you may have worked out from the name, it has something of a nautical theme, with pictures of old maps on the wall, but there's deer, venison and rabbit as well as piscatorial fare. In summer, live jazz or soul music every night and weekend lunchtimes adds to the convivial vibe created by the welcoming owner. ⓐ Kej Oslobodjenja 43, Zemun ⓣ 011 210 3950 ⓛ 09.00–01.00

Platani ££ One of the many places on Kej Oslobodjenja serving fish and meat mains, with an Italian angle. ⓐ Kej Oslobodjenja 45, Zemun ⓣ 011 210 1401 ⓛ 09.00–24.00

Žabar £££ Raft restaurant which attracts Belgrade's upper crust, so the prices are accordingly high, but ordinary locals also turn up in large groups for a special treat. Fish is the highlight on the menu, as with the other establishments in the

area. @ Kej Oslobodjenja bb, Zemun ⓣ 011 319 1226 ⓦ www.
zabar.co.rs ⓛ 12.00–24.00

BARS & CLUBS
Acapulco Unintentionally hilarious nightclub, where scantily
attired young women pair up with Belgrade toughs to the
strains of the city's ever-popular turbo-folk. Not the most
edifying of nights out, but quite fun if you don't mind the
frisson of danger from the insalubrious clientele.
@ Bulevar Nikole Tesle, Zemun ⓣ 063 778 4760
ⓛ 12.00–03.00

Bibis High-end floating café-cum-club with athletic types
both in photos on the wall and frequenting the club itself.
@ Bulevar Nikole Tesle, Zemun ⓣ 011 319 2150 ⓛ 10.00–02.00

THEATRE
Madlenianum Opera & Theatre Modern and professional
venue hosting opera, ballet, drama and classical music.
See the website for details – you can also book online.
Maximum ticket price is around 600 dinars, 800 for a seat in a
private box. There are discounts for groups. @ Glavna 32,
Zemun ⓣ 011 316 2797 ⓦ www.madlenianum.rs
ⓛ Box office: 10.00–20.00 Mon–Fri, 10.00–14.00 Sat,
17.00–20.00 Sat & Sun (performance days)

ACCOMMODATION

HOTELS

Hotel Skala ££ An intimate and low-key Zemun hotel, with just 14 rooms. Exterior, interior and staff are equally charming, and there's a well-regarded restaurant on site. ⓐ Bežanijska 3 ⓣ 011 307 5032

Hotel Continental £££ No longer part of the InterContinental chain (hence the disappearance of the 'Inter' from its name), standards are said to have slipped somewhat at this place, whose lobby was the scene of the assassination of the Serbian warlord Arkan. However, it retains its five-star ranking and a raft of facilities. ⓐ Vladimira Popovica 10, Novi Beograd ⓣ 011 220 4204 ⓦ www.continentalhotelbeograd.com

Hyatt Regency Belgrade £££ One of the city's top hotels, with bright and airy rooms, restaurants and halls that are a world away from the dreary Communist-style hotels elsewhere in the city. The entire place exudes taste, comfort and class. ⓐ Milentija Popovica 5, Novi Beograd ⓣ 011 301 1234 ⓦ www.belgrade. regency.hyatt.com

CAMPSITE

Dunav camp £ All kinds of campers are catered for, with space for tents and buses – plus bungalows available. ⓐ Cara Dusana 49, Zemun ⓣ 011 316 0256 ⓦ www.amkjedinstvo.rs ⓘ Cash only

Belgrade to Novi Sad

Although Novi Sad, which lies 80 km (50 miles) northwest of Belgrade, is Serbia's second city, don't expect a heaving metropolis. It's a university town and much of the centre is closed off to vehicles, which adds to its easy, quiet charm. Most of the buildings are small and Baroque style. There is one large building: the Petrovaradin Fortress, which lies across the Danube in its own town, and is the area's most famous monument.

The journey from Belgrade, whether you go by road or rail, also takes you near several other points of interest. Fruška Gora National Park is notable not only for pleasant scenery and the tranquillity that makes it the home of so many endangered and protected animal and plant species, but also for the 16 isolated monasteries, one of which is around 900 years old. Heading on from the national park towards Novi Sad, you'll reach the historical town of Sremski Karlovci, which for a small place has a variety of interesting architecture and makes for a pleasant stop-off point on your way between Belgrade and Novi Sad.

GETTING THERE

It's quite possible to visit Novi Sad and the stops on the way in a day trip from the capital – particularly if you have access to a car. With your own transport you could comfortably pack in some of the monasteries of Fruška Gora National Park, spend some time in the town itself and drive back after dinner.

If you don't have a car, the best option is to take the bus from the Beograd bus station, which should take 1$\frac{1}{2}$ hours to go direct to Novi Sad. A return ticket costs around 700 dinars and you will get a metal token, or *zheton*, which you have to place into a turnstile to get to your bus. Trains also make the journey, although they are slightly slower. Note that the last train leaves Novi Sad at 22.27, some three hours after the second-to-last one, while the bus keeps running until midnight. Buses in Serbia are generally more pleasant than trains.

Another option is to take a guided tour from Belgrade, which will take in Fruška Gora and other places of interest en route. The 'Romance' train travels between Belgrade and Sremski Karlovci (see page 118). If you're on an extended visit, it's worth staying

◆ *One of Fruška Gora's many monasteries*

overnight, as there are plenty of things to see (plus hotels are far better value than in Belgrade). Novi Sad is the capital of the autonomous province of Vojvodina, and you will certainly feel the difference in character and atmosphere.

SIGHTS & ATTRACTIONS

Monasteries

To see the monasteries, which are spread out over a 10 by 50 km (6 by 31 mile) area, you really need your own transport or to go as part of an organised trip – unless you're prepared to spend a lot of time negotiating rural Serbian buses. The monasteries certainly repay your effort in getting there: dating back as far as the 12th century, they are beautiful monuments to Orthodoxy; collections of icons are often on display inside. The Novi Sad tourist office will be able to give further details.

Novi Sad tourist office ⓐ Modene 1 ❶ 021 661 7344 ⓔ info@ turizamns.rs ⓛ 07.30–20.00 Mon–Fri, 10.00–15.00 Sat

Nacionalni Park Fruška Gora (Fruška Gora National Park)

Taking its name from the mountain, Fruška Gora is about one main thing: isolation. The inhabitants, be they the endangered species of plant, animal and bird that seek sanctuary in the loneliness here, or the inmates of the 16 monasteries in the area, have found a refuge away from the hustle and bustle of Serbia. Some 22.5 sq km (9 sq miles) is protected area, and it's clear why locals know the region as the jewel of Vojvodina.

The park covers a large area and you may choose to base yourself in the park itself for a couple of days – the website below includes details of accommodation and restaurants. As well as just enjoying the tranquillity and scenery, you can also hike, cycle, fish and even hunt. A tourist information centre and museum at Iriski Venac recently opened, and information is always available either by phone or on the park's comprehensive website. **ⓐ** Zmajev trg 1, Sremska Kamenica **ⓣ** 021 463 666 **ⓦ** www.npfruskagora.co.rs

Petrovaradinska Tvrdava (Petrovaradin Fortress)

Built by the Romans and with alterations by all of the groups who succeeded them, Petrovaradin Fortress stands proudly overlooking the Danube. Although peacetime has rendered it redundant, it's still an impressive structure with 18 km (11 miles) of galleries beneath the fortress, over half of which are accessible to the public via guided tour – make sure you give plenty of advance notice if you wish to take advantage of this. Today it houses the Muzej Grada Novog Sada (City Museum), a collection of art and artefacts from the past two centuries, plus a planetarium and observatory, but it is perhaps most famous for hosting the EXIT festival (see box on page 122). **ⓐ** Strosmajerova **ⓣ** Fortress: 021 643 3145; planetarium: 021 485 2826 **ⓛ** Fortress: 09.00–17.00 Tues–Sun; planetarium: 19.00–24.00 Sat **ⓝ** Bus: 3

Sremski Karlovci

The quiet historical town of Sremski Karlovci has something of a collegiate feel to it. Just 11 km (7 miles) southeast of Novi Sad, it's easy to combine with a trip to Serbia's second city. All the main buildings are on Trg Branka Radičevića, the tree-lined central square. The town's chief point of interest is its architecture –

by standing in the middle of Trg Branka Radičevića you can see neoclassical, traditional Serbian, Secessionist and neo-Byzantine features. Some of the buildings, such as the museum and main gallery, are also worth a look.

Cultural Centre Gallery @ Trg Branka Radičevića 7 ☏ 021 881 075 🕒 09.00–16.00 Mon–Sat during exhibitions only

Museum @ Patrijarha Rajačića 16 ☏ 021 881 637 🕒 09.00–17.00 Mon–Sat

One interesting way of getting to Sremski Karlovci is by the so-called 'Romance' train from Belgrade, which makes the journey to the town and back on Saturdays and sometimes Sundays between spring and autumn, leaving Belgrade in the morning and returning early evening (journey time of about 90 minutes). The exact departure times are wont to change, so check ahead. Tickets, which range from about 300 to 700 dinars, can be bought from Belgrade and Novi Sad stations as well as travel agencies.

● *The Orthodox seminary is one of Sremski Karlovci's architectural gems*

Other activities in the area include wine tasting, and there is plenty of information about this and other attractions on the town's website. Staff at the small tourist information office, which also has a gift shop with books and a decent array of Serbian wine on sale, will be happy to furnish you with maps and tell you about the town. They also have a lot of information on Fruška Gora.
ⓐ Patrijarha Rajačića 1 ⓣ 021 883 855 ⓦ www.karlovci.org.rs

AFTER DARK

RESTAURANTS

Boem ££ Grand, old-fashioned hotel-restaurant with mostly meat and fish dishes and a few pasta meals. ⓐ Trg Branka Radičevića 5, Sremski Karlovci ⓣ 021 881 038

Vila Prezident ££ A lovely location, warm wooden interior, hearty Serbian fare, occasional live music and a wine cellar, all recommend this hotel restaurant. ⓐ Belilo 71 (on the way to Strazilovo) ⓣ 021 883 325/063 882 0119 ⓦ www.vilaprezident.com

Novi Sad

With its appealing Baroque architecture, car-free centre and small-town vibe, Serbia's second city is totally different from its first. It's actually a capital itself, of the autonomous province Vojvodina. It's also a university town, and enjoys that carefree atmosphere that only students can create. Your starting point is likely to be Trg Slobode, a large and impressive square that feels like something out of a glamorous European film, dominated by the Roman Catholic St Mary's Church. It's a striking building, even more so at night when gloriously lit up. Across from St Mary's is another impressive edifice, City Hall.

Walking in the opposite direction from there you'll be on the neatly paved Zmaj Jovina, also barred to traffic, which seems almost entirely given over to cafés and restaurants, and the odd designer clothes shop. When the weather is warm enough, the pavement is thronged with tables.

You'll find that the local people are only too happy to help if you need guidance around town.

SIGHTS & ATTRACTIONS

Dunavska Park

Well-tended city park with a pond, statues and benches.
ⓐ Between Dunavska & Bulevar Mihaila Pupina

CULTURE

Francuski institut u Srbiji (French Institute in Serbia)

Details of the various events and festivals the institute (previously known as the French Cultural Centre) organises are available on the website. It's in French (and Serbian) but you should be able to get the idea. ⓐ Pašićeva 33 ⓣ 021 472 2900 ⓦ www.ccfns.org.rs ⓛ 13.00–20.00 Mon–Fri

Zbirka Strane Umetnosti Muzeja Grada Novog Sada (City Museum of Novi Sad – Foreign Art Collection)

The gallery houses the biggest collection of foreign art in the country, from Renaissance to modern, the majority of which

is from continental Europe. ⓐ Dunavska 29 ⓣ 021 451 239
ⓦ www.museumns.rs ⓛ 10.00–17.00 Tues–Sun, 14.00–20.00 Sat
ⓘ Admission charge

Muzej Vojvodine (Vojvodina Museum)

Two separate buildings containing a plethora of items and
displays related to the province. One collection is devoted
to archaeology and culture; more recent history, including a
section on World War II, is covered next door. ⓐ Dunavska 35–37
ⓣ 021 420 566 ⓦ www.muzejvojvodine.org.rs ⓛ 10.00–18.00
Tues–Fri, 10.00–18.00 Sat & Sun ⓘ Admission charge

◬ Novi Sad's City Museum houses a comprehensive art collection

EXIT FESTIVAL

Novi Sad's EXIT music festival started out in 2000 as a student protest against Slobodan Milošević and has developed into such a cult event that – when there was no Glastonbury in 2006 – the *Guardian* newspaper named it best festival. It now attracts up to a quarter of a million people and headline acts such as Franz Ferdinand, Arcade Fire, Pulp, Lily Allen and Arctic Monkeys. Despite some unfortunate dramas over the years, including the organisers being arrested for embezzlement and performers being pelted with missiles, the summer festival has gone from strength to strength and is now feted in the international press, attracting a huge foreign contingent, lured by tickets which cost considerably less than they would do at comparable events elsewhere. ⓦ www.exitfest.org

TAKING A BREAK

Art Fusion £ A gallery and café rolled into one, this small, cosy and brightly lit venue holds exhibitions of local artists' latest projects and has Internet access as well. ⓐ Laze Teleckog 7 ⓣ 064 151 3605 ⓛ 10.00–23.00 Sun–Fri, 10.00–01.00 Sat

Nublu £ Artsy establishment that is also home to a gallery and bookshop. ⓐ Žarka Zrenjanina 12 ⓣ 021 525 365 ⓦ www.nublu.rs ⓛ 09.30–23.00 Mon–Thur, 09.30–01.00 Fri & Sat, 16.00–23.00 Sun

Radio Café £ A typically laid-back Novi Sad atmosphere is augmented by an impressive array of old radios. There is also a real radio station at work upstairs as well as a downstairs bookshop. ⓐ Svetozara Miletića 45 ⓣ 021 520 735 ⓛ 08.00–23.00 Sun–Thur, 08.00–01.00 Fri & Sat

AFTER DARK

Restaurants

A lot of Novi Sad's restaurants are along Zmaj Jovina and Nikole Pašića, which is also known as Pašićeva.

Gusan £ A good range of reasonably priced local fare on offer here, in what becomes a refuge for the tired hordes attending the EXIT festival during the summer. ⓐ Zmaj Jovina 4 ⓣ 021 425 570 ⓦ www.pivnicagusan.com (Serbian) ⓛ 08.00–24.00

Arhiv ££ Cosy and smart restaurant with a tunnel roof, where helpful staff serve national and international cuisine. ⓐ Ilije Ognjanovića 16 ⓣ 021 472 2176 ⓛ 09.00–23.00 Mon–Sat

Fontana ££ Highly rated restaurant at the hotel of the same name, with Serbian and international dishes served by friendly staff, often to a background of live music. In summer the courtyard and fountain are particularly pleasant. ⓐ Nikole Pašića 27 ⓣ 021 661 2760 ⓦ www.restoranfontana.com (Serbian)

Pomodoro Rosso ££ Complemented by mellow music and a warm red and wood interior, Pomodoro Rosso offers an Italian trattoria

menu with great service and great atmosphere. ⓐ Pašićeva 14
ⓣ 021 424 023 ⓦ www.pomodororosso.com ⓛ 14.00–23.00

Cercil (Churchill) £££ Three restaurants under one roof, providing
Italian and Serbian cuisine with French and Italian wines, plus
pastries in the café. The service is friendly and attentive.
ⓐ Pašićeva 25 ⓣ 021 525 132 ⓛ 08.00–23.00 Mon–Sat

Bars & clubs
London Club There is no mistaking the Anglophile sentiments
of this pub-cum-club. It used to house a red telephone box, but
that is now in the bar across the street. Live music downstairs.
ⓐ Laze Teleckog 3 ⓣ 021 421 881 ⓛ 09.00–02.00 Sun–Thur,
09.00–03.00 Fri & Sat

ACCOMMODATION

Prezident Hotel £ With both indoor and outdoor pools, plush
comfortable rooms and friendly staff, Novi Sad's first five-star
hotel offers such extraordinary value for money you might
consider commuting to Belgrade from here. A current refit
should see it emerge looking even better. ⓐ Futoška 9
ⓣ 021 487 7444 ⓦ www.prezidenthotel.com

Vojvodina £ Right on the main square, the city's oldest hotel
has large, bright rooms and offers good value for money.
ⓐ Trg Slobode 2 ⓣ 021 662 2122 ⓦ www.hotelvojvodina.rs

◐ *Pointing you in the right direction*

Belgrade Cultural Centre

Skadarlija - bohemian quarter

Галерија "Графички колектив"

Republic Square

PRACTICAL
information

Directory

GETTING THERE
By air

Low-cost airlines have made huge inroads into Belgrade in recent years, with Wizz Air starting up a route from London Luton that goes three or four times a week, for as little as £70 return if you book well in advance. It's also possible to reach Belgrade through a combination of cheap flights, such as from London Stansted–Cologne and from Cologne–Belgrade with Germanwings. Another option is to take a cheap flight to somewhere nearby such as Budapest, Bucharest, Ljubljana, Sofia or somewhere in neighbouring Croatia with easyJet, Ryanair or Wizz Air, and continue by land.

easyJet Ⓦ www.easyjet.com ❶ 0843 104 5000

Germanwings ❶ 0906 294 1918 Ⓦ www.germanwings.com ❷ 05.00–22.00

Ryanair ❶ 0871 246 0000 Ⓦ www.ryanair.com ❷ 09.00–19.00 Mon–Fri, 10.00–17.00 Sat, 11.00–17.00 Sun

Wizz Air ❶ 0906 959 0002 Ⓦ www.wizzair.com

If you prefer to go by the express route, British Airways and Serbian national carrier JAT run direct flights, taking just under three hours.

British Airways ❶ 0870 850 9850 Ⓦ www.ba.com ❷ 06.00–20.00

JAT ❶ 020 7629 2007 Ⓦ www.jat.com ❷ 09.30–17.30 Mon–Fri

Other major airlines, including Lufthansa, Czech Airlines, Austrian Airlines, Air France and Alitalia, offer cheaper flights from the UK with a stopover, but you won't save much.

Many people are aware that travel emits CO_2, which contributes to climate change. You may be interested in the possibility of lessening the environmental impact of your flight through the charity **Climate Care** (w www.climatecare.org), which offsets your CO_2 by funding environmental projects around the world.

By rail

If you don't mind several changes, you can reach the Serbian capital by train from the UK, though it's no cheaper than flying with a traditional carrier, and rather more expensive than with a low-cost airline. Trains tend to get cheaper the further east you go, so getting a cheap flight to a nearby city and picking up the train from there could work out better value.

European Rail t 020 7387 0444 w www.europeanrail.com
Thomas Cook European Rail Timetable t 01733 416 477
w www.thomascookpublishing.com
TrainsEurope t 0871 700 7722 w www.trainseurope.co.uk

By road

With its limited departure days, near 40-hour journey and comparable cost to the plane, the bus has little to recommend it, but you could fly part-way and continue by road.

Eurolines t 08717 818181 w www.eurolines.co.uk c 24 hours
Lasta (Eurolines' Serbian affiliate) t 0800 334 334
w www.lasta.rs

If you're driving yourself, then the optimum driving route goes via France, Belgium, Germany, Austria, Slovenia and Croatia and takes around 24 hours of road time. Be warned that Serbia is not the best-signposted country in Europe. Highway tolls are not exorbitant, though, and are the same for foreign and domestic cars, and it's possible to pay in euros or by credit card.

ENTRY FORMALITIES

UK, Irish, EU, US, Canadian, Australian and New Zealand citizens can stay for up to 90 days in Serbia without a visa. South Africans do need a visa and should apply to their local Serbian embassy with their passport, letter of invitation (which can be from a Serbian travel agency), return ticket and proof of sufficient funds and medical insurance.

Make sure you get a stamp in your passport on entry. You are technically supposed to register with the local police within 24 hours of reaching your destination – if you're staying in a hotel, they will do this for you. You are obliged to declare any sums over €5,000 on arrival.

MONEY

The Serbian currency is the dinar, which comes in notes of 10, 20, 50, 100, 200, 500, 1,000 and 5,000 dinars and coins of 1, 2, 5, 10 and 20 dinars. Within Belgrade, bureaux de change are fairly

TRAVEL INSURANCE

Britain has a reciprocal healthcare agreement with Serbia, which theoretically means that all emergency treatment should be free, but taking out medical insurance before you leave is still strongly recommended.

ubiquitous, and some stay open until 23.00. Banks and post offices will also change foreign currency, and special money-changing machines are in service 24 hours a day. Rates do not vary much and charging commission is illegal, unless you have traveller's cheques, which fewer places will cash.

ATMs are fairly easy to find in Belgrade, but not all machines accept every kind of card, so if you have more than one type, bring them all. Credit cards are increasingly accepted in the better hotels, restaurants and shops, but carry around some cash in case.

HEALTH, SAFETY & CRIME

Belgrade poses few health risks to the visitor, although you should take out adequate medical insurance prior to your trip. No specific jabs are required and Belgrade's tap water is safe to drink. Although Belgrade's hospitals and healthcare system may seem a little basic, Serbian doctors are generally highly trained. However, avoid petting stray dogs – a very small number of rabid ones have been reported – and seek help immediately if you get bitten.

Belgrade today is relatively free from violence. While Serbia does suffer from its fair share of organised crime, this is unlikely to affect tourists. That said, it is not an affluent country, and foreign tourists may be targeted by thieves. Take all the usual precautions that you do when abroad – keep your money in a safe place, don't flaunt valuables and expensive jewellery and avoid any areas that seem threatening. Take extra care if you're driving an expensive vehicle.

The city's police force maintains a significant presence throughout the city, often checking that Belgrade's myriad of confusing traffic rules are being respected. Serbian police have something of a reputation for corruption, and sometimes target foreign drivers in the hope of soliciting a bribe, although things have improved a great deal in this respect. Taking photos of the police, their vehicles or any kind of military facility is not a good idea.

OPENING HOURS

Belgrade's shops and bureaux de change are usually open from 08.00 to 20.00 Monday to Friday and from 08.00 to 15.00 Saturday, but in the centre of town they often stay open much later, until 22.00 or 23.00. Grocery stores and supermarkets also tend to keep longer hours. Smaller businesses sometimes close for lunch and many places stay shut on public holidays. Markets operate on a more ad hoc basis.

Banks are open from 08.00 to 19.00 on weekdays and 08.00 to 15.00 on Saturdays. A handful are also open on Sundays.

Museums and attractions tend to open at 09.00 or 10.00 and close at 17.00 from Tuesday to Friday; Monday is the usual closing day. On Thursday a lot of places open and close later, from around 12.00 until 20.00. On Sunday the larger attractions are open from 09.00 or 10.00 to 13.00 or 14.00, while the smaller ones remain closed. On Saturday some places open to their weekday schedule, others have a more limited programme and the smaller ones stay shut. Public holidays also result in some closures.

TOILETS

While bars, restaurants, hotels and petrol stations all have clean and adequate conveniences, the public ones can be hit and miss

— and you'd do well to take some toilet paper with you just in case. On the plus side, it shouldn't be too difficult to find one.

CHILDREN
It might not be the obvious holiday destination if you have children in tow, but Belgrade is surprisingly geared up for kids and you'll find children's playgrounds all over the place. Serbia

○ *There are plenty of different entertainment options for children*

is a child-friendly nation and your little ones will be welcome in most places. You can pick up baby food and nappies without problem in Belgrade's chemists and supermarkets.

In the warmer months, Kalemegdan is a great family favourite, with plenty of room to kick around a ball and lots of climbable statues. Early October brings the **Joy of Europe festival** (☎ 011 323 2043 ⓦ www.joyofeurope.rs), a week-long event in which 7- to 14-year-olds from all over Europe come to Belgrade to participate in various concerts, processions, contests, shows and exhibitions.

In the last two weeks of December, Belgrade Fair plays host to an amusement park, concerts and food, both for the young and for the young at heart.

COMMUNICATIONS
Internet
Internet cafés with decent connection speeds can be found in Belgrade; though, as elsewhere, free Wi-Fi is becoming ever more available and many places, including hotels, restaurants and cafés, advertise it (though whether it works or not is another matter!) ❶ Note that the domain '.yu' was finally phased out in 2010 and replaced by '.rs'.

Phone
The city has good mobile coverage and, provided you have activated international roaming, your phone should work fine. If you do need to make calls from public phones, one way is to visit a post office and use its telephone centre – at the city's main post offices these centres are accessible after the normal

TELEPHONING SERBIA

To make an international call to Serbia, dial 00, followed by the country code (381), followed by the phone number, omitting the initial zero.

TELEPHONING ABROAD

To make an international call from Serbia, dial 00, followed by the country code, followed by the phone number you require, usually omitting the initial zero. Some country codes are: Australia 61, New Zealand 64, Republic of Ireland 353, South Africa 27, UK 44, USA and Canada 1

post office opening hours. You make your call from a private booth and pay afterwards.

Main Post Office telephone centre ⓐ Tavoska 2, near Sveti Marko Church ⓛ 07.00–24.00 Mon–Fri, 07.00–22.00 Sat & Sun

Central Post Office telephone centre ⓐ Zmaj Jovina 17 ⓛ 07.00–22.00

The other way is to buy a Halo card (*Halo kartica*) from a post office or kiosk and look for a red phone booth, of which there are many, on the street. Dialling out from your hotel room is as extortionate in Belgrade as it is elsewhere.

Post

While Serbia's postal service is reliable, if you're sending anything of vital importance it's better to use a courier service. Post offices are open from 08.00 to 19.00 on weekdays and 08.00 to 15.00 on Saturdays. A few also open on Sundays. Sending a postcard to the UK, Ireland or the rest of Europe costs 46 dinar; letters start from the same price and go upwards according to weight. Mail should arrive within three to five days, longer if the destination is outside Europe. Postboxes, regal-looking maroon objects with gold trimmings, are relatively easy to find in the city centre.

ELECTRICITY

Serbia's electricity supply is at 220V AC. Plugs are of the round two-pin variety used in continental Europe, so if you're bringing appliances from outside the region you'll need an adaptor, which you can pick up at the airport.

TRAVELLERS WITH DISABILITIES

Given that facilities for travellers with disabilities within Europe generally become worse the further east you go, getting around Belgrade is not as difficult as you might expect, although you'll have to contend with uneven street surfaces, cars blocking the pavement and some reckless driving. Attitudes have improved a lot recently and the city has spent money on improving its infrastructure and making itself more accessible. There are ramps in several of the main buildings and the central pedestrianised area is flat and smooth. Most of the better hotels have at least a few rooms that are suitable for guests with disabilities. Avoid the Skadarlija district, where steep cobbles test even the able-bodied.

The Tourist Organisation of Belgrade also publishes an extensive guide for tourists with disabilities, which covers attractions, areas, hotels and restaurants, and includes details such as ramps, revolving doors, lifts and so on. It can be downloaded from ⓦ www.tob.rs

Tourism for All is a charity that advocates for accessible tourism, and provides advice on planning a holiday. 🅦 www.tourismforall.org.uk

TOURIST INFORMATION

The **Tourist Organisation of Belgrade** posts a comprehensive list of events in the city on its website. It can also book you on various trips, including riverboat cruises. 🅐 Knez Mihailova 6 🅣 011 328 1859 🅦 www.tob.rs 🅛 09.00–21.00 Mon–Sat, 10.00–15.00 Sun

Tourist information centres can be found in the city centre at: 🅐 Central Railway Station 🅣 011 361 2732 🅛 08.00–20.00 Mon–Fri, 09.00–16.00 Sat & Sun
🅐 Sava Pier, Karađorđeva 🅣 011 328 8246 🅛 08.00–19.00 (Mar–Nov)
There is also an office at the airport 🅣 011 209 7638
🅛 09.00–22.00

Information on the rest of the country is available from the **National Tourist Organisation of Serbia** 🅐 Cika Ljubina 8/1 🅣 021 472 4088 🅦 www.visitserbia.org 🅛 08.00–20.00 Mon–Fri, 09.00–17.00 Sat, 10.00–16.00 Sun

BACKGROUND READING

The colossal book *Black Lamb and Grey Falcon: A Journey through Yugoslavia* by Rebecca West traces the author's travels through the country in the run-up to World War II. It's an absorbing read for anyone interested in Yugoslavia and, at over a thousand pages, is likely to keep you going for most of your trip.

Emergencies

EMERGENCY NUMBERS
General emergency 🕿 112   **Police** 🕿 92
Fire brigade 🕿 93   **Medical emergency** 🕿 94

MEDICAL SERVICES
The facilities might look rather primitive, but Serbian medical
professionals are typically very well trained. If you need a doctor,
first contact your hotel reception. Failing that, go to hospital or
call the emergency number 🕿 94. Many doctors will speak English.

Hospitals
Kliniki Centar (Clinical Centre of Serbia) 🏠 Pasterova 2
🕿 011 361 7777 🌐 www.kcs.ac.rs (Serbian)
Urgenti Centar (Emergency Centre) 🏠 Pasterova 2 🕿 011 361 8444

Private, English-speaking clinics
Poliklinika Bel Medic 🏠 Viktora Igoa 1 🕿 011 309 1000
🌐 http://belmedic.rs 🕘 24 hours
Poliklinika Dr Ristic 🏠 Narodnih Heroja 38 🕿 011 269 3287
🌐 www.dr-ristic.com 🕘 24 hours

Dentists
An English-speaking dentist can be found at **Beldent** 🏠 Brankova 23
🕿 011 263 4455 🌐 www.beldent.rs
There are a couple of dentists open 24 hours:
🏠 Obilic Venac 30 🕿 011 263 5236
🏠 Kneginje Zorke 🕿 011 244 1413

EMERGENCY PHRASES

Fire!	**Help!**	**Stop!**
Požar!	Pomoći!	Stop!
Pozhar!	*Pomoch!*	*Stop!*

Call the fire brigade/the police/an ambulance!
Pozovite vatrogasce/policiju/hitnu pomoć!
Pozoveete vatrogasce/poleeceeyoo/heetnoo pomoch!

Pharmacies
Prima I is open permanently. ⓐ Nemanjina 2 ☎ 011 361 1088

Police
In an emergency, ask for help from your hotel staff; otherwise call ☎ 92. There is a special **Foreigners' Police Department** in the Interior Ministry. ⓐ Savska 35 ☎ 011 361 8956

EMBASSIES & CONSULATES
Australia ⓐ 8th floor, Vladimira Popovića 38–40, Novi Beograd
☎ 021 330 3400 🖥 www.serbia.embassy.gov.au
Canada ⓐ Kneza Miloša 7 ☎ 011 306 3000 🖥 www.serbia.gc.ca
UK ⓐ Resavska 46 ☎ 011 264 5055 🖥 www.ukinserbia.fco.gov.uk
US ⓐ Kneza Miloša 50 ☎ 011 361 9344 🖥 http://serbia.usembassy.gov
Irish citizens are entitled to the assistance of other EU member state embassies.

A

accommodation 34–9
  Novi Beograd
    & Zemun 113
  Novi Sad 124
Ada Ciganlija 32, 88, 92
air travel 48–9, 126–7
alcohol 27
Applied Art Museum
  69–70
arts *see* culture

B

background reading 135
Bajlonijeva Pijaca 83–4
Bajrakli Dzamija
  (Mosque) 58–9, 62
Banjica Concentration
  Camp Museum 98
bars & clubs *see* nightlife
Belgrade Fair 98–9
Belgrade Summer
  Festival 12–13
Belgrade Zoo 62
Beogradski Sajam 98–9
Beogradski
  Zoološki vrt 62
Birčaninova 95
BITEF Teatar (Theatre) 87
bombed buildings 83
Botanickoj basti
  Jevremovac 92
bunker 98
bus travel 48, 53–6, 102,
  114–15, 127

C

cafés 27
  Kalemegdan area 71–2
  Novi Sad 122–3
  South Belgrade 99
  Trg Republike area 84–5
  Zemun 110
camping 113
car hire 56
Centar za Grafiku
  i Vizeulna Istrazivanja
  68
Centre for Graphic Art
  & Visual Research 68
children 20, 64, 131–2
cinema 31, 46, 82–3
city centre 76–87
City Museum of Novi
  Sad – Foreign Art
  collection 120–21
clock tower 64
consulates 137
crime 53, 129–30
cruises 109
culture 12–13, 18–20, 31,
  44–5, 46
Cvijeta Zuzorić
  Art Pavilion 70–71

D

dentists 136
disabilities 134–5
driving 52–3, 56, 102, 114,
  127–8
Dunavska Park 120

E

electricity 134
embassies 95, 137
emergencies 136–7
entertainment 29–31
  see also nightlife
Ethnographic Museum
  68–9
Etno Muzej 68–9
events 8–13, 29–31,
  44–5, 98–9, 106–8, 122,
  132
EXIT Festival 117, 122

F

Federal Parliament
  building 77, 80
festivals 8–13, 122, 132
floating & riverside
  venues 29, 108, 111–12
food & drink 25–8
football 32–3, 93–4
Francuski institut u
  Srbiji 120
French Institute in Serbia
  120
Fresco Gallery 69
Fruška Gora
  National Park 116–17

G

Galerija Fresaka 69

H

Hala Pionir 32, 97
Hala Sportova 32, 109

health 129, 136–7
history 14–15, 80, 83, 97–8
Holy Archangel
   Michael Church 67
hotels *see* accommodation
House of Flowers 92–3

I
Ilije Garašanina 99
insurance 128
Internet 132

J
Jevrejski Istorijski Muzej
   69
Jevremovac
   Botanical Gardens 92
Jewish Historical
   Museum 69
Joy of Europe festival 132

K
Kalemegdan Tvrdjava
   (Fortress) 58, 62, 64
Kalemegdan Fortress area
   58–75
Kalenić Pijaca 99
Knez Mihailova 58, 65, 71
Konak Kneginje Ljubice
   65, 67
Kuća Cveća 92–3

L
language 24, 28, 52, 138
lifestyle 16–17
listings 20, 31, 135

M
Madlenianum Opera
   & Theatre 112
malls 22
markets 24, 64, 83–4,
   98–9, 106
Messenger of Victory
   monument 62–4
Military Museum 71
Milošević, Slobodan 15,
   80, 98
monasteries 116
money 128–9
Museum of Contemporary
   Art 109–10
Museum of the Serbian
   Orthodox Church
   69–70
Museum of Yugoslav
   Cinema 82–3
music 20, 29–31, 75,
   106–8, 112
Muzej Jugoslavenska
   Kinoteka 82–3
Muzej nad Koncentracijski
   logor Banjica 98
Muzej nad Odredeni
   Clan Srpski Pravoslavan
   Crkva 69–70
Muzej Primenjene
   Umetnosti 70
Muzej Savremene
   Umetnosti 109–10
Muzej Vojvodine 121

Muzej Zemun 110

N
Nacionalni Park
   Fruška Gora 116–17
Narodno Pozoriste
   18–20, 87
National Theatre 18–20,
   87
NATO campaign
   monument 97
Natural History
   Museum Gallery 70
New Belgrade 102–13
nightlife 29–31
   Kalemegdan area 75
   Novi Beograd 106–8
   Novi Sad 124
   South Belgrade 100
   Trg Republike area 86–7
   Zemun 112
Novi Beograd 102–13
Novi Sad 114, 119–24

O
opening hours 130
Orthodox Cathedral 67
Orthodox church 67, 69,
   95–7, 102–6, 116–17

P
parks & gardens 44, 62–4,
   67–8, 92, 97–8, 116–17
Parliament 77–80
Partizan Belgrade 32–3,
   93–4

passports & visas 128
Petrovaradinska Tvrdava
    (Fortress) 117
pharmacies 137
phones 132–3
picnicking 28
Pobednik 62–4
police 129–30, 137
post 133–4
Princess Ljubica's Konak
    65, 67
Prirodnjacki Muzej 70
public holidays 11
public transport 48, 52,
    53–6, 102, 114–15, 127–8

R
rail travel 52, 56, 102, 115,
    118, 127
Red Star Belgrade 32–3,
    93–4
restaurants 25–8
    Kalemegdan area 72,
        74–5
    Novi Sad 123–4
    South Belgrade 100
    Sremski Karlovci 119
    Trg Republike area 85–6
    Zemun 111–12

S
Saborna crkva
    Sv Arhangela 67
safety 53, 129–30

St Mark's Church 95
St Mary's Church 120
St Sava's Church 95–7
Savezni Skupstina zgrada
    77, 80
seasons 8
Seik Mustafino Turbe 67
Serbian Academy of
    Sciences & Arts 75
Sheik Mustafa's Tomb 67
shopping 22–4, 46
    Kalemegdan area 71
    South Belgrade 98–9
    Trg Republike area 83–4
Skadarlija (Skadarska) 22,
    24, 80–81
smoking 16
South Belgrade 88–100
sport & activities 32–3
Sremski Karlovci 117–18
street of embassies 95
Students' Cultural Centre
    98
Studentski Kulturni
    Centar 98
Sveta Marka 95
Sveti Sava 95–7
symbols & abbreviations 4

T
Tašmajdan Park 97
taxis 48–9, 56
Terazije 76, 81–2

Terazije Fountain 82
theatre 18–20, 31, 87, 112
time difference 48
tipping 28
Tito Memorial Complex
    92–3
toilets 130–31
Topčider Park 97–8
tourist information 135
tours 115, 118–19
trams 53–6
Trg Republike 76, 82
Trg Studentski 67–8
trolleybuses 53–6
turbo-folk 107

U
Umetnicki paviljon
    Cvijeta Zuzorić 70–71

V
Vojni Muzej 71
Vojvodina Museum 121

W
weather 8, 46–7

Z
Zbirka Strane Umetnosti
    Muzeja Grada Novog
    Sada 120–21
Zemun 102–13
Zemun Museum 110
Zmaj Jovina 120, 123
zoo 62

ACKNOWLEDGEMENTS

Thomas Cook Publishing wishes to thank VASILE SZAKACS, to whom the copyright belongs, for the photographs in this book, except for the following images:

Balkan hotel, page 35; Belgrade Cultural Network, page 9; Julija Sapic/BigStockPhoto.com, page 131; Elena Sherman/ BigStockPhoto.com, page 59; Djordje Tomic, page 13; World Pictures/ Photoshot, pages 21, 40–41 & 49.

For CAMBRIDGE PUBLISHING MANAGEMENT LIMITED:
Project editor: Karen Beaulah
Layout: Donna Pedley
Proofreaders: Penny Isaac & Jan McCann

Send your thoughts to
books@thomascook.com

- Found a great bar, club, shop or must-see sight that we don't feature?
- Like to tip us off about any information that needs a little updating?
- Want to tell us what you love about this handy little guidebook and more importantly how we can make it even handier?

Then here's your chance to tell all! Send us ideas, discoveries and recommendations today and then look out for your valuable input in the next edition of this title.

Email the above address (stating the title) or write to:
pocket guides Series Editor, Thomas Cook Publishing, PO Box 227, Coningsby Road, Peterborough PE3 8SB, UK.

WHAT'S IN YOUR GUIDEBOOK?

Independent authors Impartial up-to-date information from our travel experts who meticulously source local knowledge.

Experience Thomas Cook's 165 years in the travel industry and guidebook publishing enriches every word with expertise you can trust.

Travel know-how Thomas Cook has thousands of staff working around the globe, all living and breathing travel.

Editors Travel-publishing professionals, pulling everything together to craft a perfect blend of words, pictures, maps and design.

You, the traveller We deliver a practical, no-nonsense approach to information, geared to how you really use it.

Useful phrases

English	Serbian	*Approx pronunciation*
BASICS		
Yes	Da	*Da*
No	Ne	*Ne*
Please	Molim	*Moleem*
Thank you	Hvala	*Hvala*
Hello	Zdravo	*Zdravo*
Goodbye	Doviđenja/ćao	*Do veejenya/ciao*
Excuse me	Izvinite	*Izveeneete*
Sorry	Pardon/izvinite	*Pardon/izveeneete*
That's OK	U redu je	*Oo-redoo ye*
I do not speak Serbian	Ne pričam srpski	*Nea preecham srpskee*
Do you speak English?	Da li pričate engleski?	*Dah-lee preechate enghleski?*
Good morning	Dobro jutro	*Dobro yootro*
Good afternoon	Dobar dan	*Dobar dan*
Good evening	Dobro veče	*Dobro veche*
Goodnight	Laku noć	*Lakoo noch*
My name is ...	Ja se zovem ...	*Ja se zovem ...*
NUMBERS		
One	Jedan	*Yedan*
Two	Dva	*Dva*
Three	Tri	*Tree*
Four	Četri	*Chetree*
Five	Pet	*Pet*
Six	Šest	*Shest*
Seven	Sedam	*Sedam*
Eight	Osam	*Osam*
Nine	Devet	*Devet*
Ten	Deset	*Deset*
Twenty	Dvadeset	*Dvadeset*
Fifty	Pedeset	*Pedeset*
One hundred	Sto	*Sto*
SIGNS & NOTICES		
Airport	Aerodrom	*Ahero-drohm*
Railway station	Železnička stanica	*Zheleznitchka stanica*
Smoking/ No smoking	Pušenje dozvoljeno/ Zabranjeno pušenje	*Pooshenye dhozvolyehno/ Zabranyeno pooshenye*
Toilets	Toalet	*Towalet*
Ladies/Gentlemen	Ženski/Muški	*Zhenski/Mooh-shki*